ARCHETYPE OF THE WOMAN PROTECTOR

A Journey to Self-Actualization

by
Dr. Kumu Michelle Manu, JD, PhD

The Archetype of the Woman Protector

Copyright 2024 Dr. Kumu Michelle Manu, JD, PhD

ISBN: 978-0-9829926-1-6 (Paperback)

All rights reserved. Printed on acid-free paper. No part of this publication may be reproduced, stored in a retrieval system, or transmitted in any form or by any means, electronic, mechanical, recording or otherwise, without the prior written permission of the author.

Published in the United States by
Five Birds Publications,
For Heroes' Hearts® Inc.
2490 EastShore Place Unit K110
Reno NV 89509

This book is not intended as libelous, slanderous or to caste a negative pall on any person either living or dead. The contents are completely derived from first person, published writings of Dr. Kumu Michelle Manu, JD, PhD.

Any opinions or statements made by the author are intended for clarification and educational purposes. To that end, some names and scenes may have been modified to protect those wishing and deserving to remain anonymous.

Edited by Gordon Richiusa
Cover Design: Jessie Buchanan
About The Author portrait: Shaan Davis
Cover Photo: James Trotter

The Archetype of the Woman Protector

Acknowledgements

Māhalo au iā 'oe

I am thankful for you

Thank you to the University of Metaphysics, Rev. L., Ph.D., and D. Callahan for your instruction, guidance, and kind support; I thank my late metaphysician, E. Burlingame, for his no-nonsense guidance and support; I thank my late Lua teacher, 'Ōlohe Solomon Kaihewalu, for feeding and trusting me with this sacred cultural and familial knowledge; I thank my invaluable mentors and teachers Kumu Lucia Tarallo and Kumu Dane Silva;

To the amazing families who took me in as their own during adolescence. I will never forget your acceptance, generosity, love, and safety you provided; I thank my trusted and supportive friends, lover, dedicated students, and hanai family that support and stand with and behind me; Thank you to my wellness and healing team, a.k.a. "life support team" – Dr. Khriech, Dr. Kim, NLP/NKT Kūkaniloko; and K. Pentecost of Wisdom Dance; Thank you to my hosts, domestic and abroad, who are led to host events where I may share metaphysical and warrior-protector principles;

Thank you to my editor, Mark Sevi (Visionstrike.com), J. Trotter, P. Ghee, D. Dye, E. Rampell, G. Richiusa of Heroes' Hearts, L. Mitchell, and Michael and Karen Matsuda of the Martial Arts History Museum.

Thank you to all those who supported me early on who have chosen to not be in my life any longer. I have learned much from you all and wish you abundance and peace.

Me ke aloha pau 'ole

With love forever

The Archetype of the Woman Protector

Contents

1. Introduction
2. My Journey
3. Warrior or Protector?
4. Protector Energy
5. The Path of the Protector
6. Metaphysical Science
7. Archetypal Energy
8. Rewriting Archetypes
9. Spirituality Within Movement
10. The Physics of Movement
11. Energies in Movement
12. Duality of Energies
13. Metaphysical Protector Energy
14. The Woman Protector
15. Embracing the Role of Protector
16. The Modern Protector
17. Conclusion

The Archetype of the Woman Protector

Introduction

"The unexamined life is not worth living."
—*Socrates*

Starting at a very young age, I can recall many instances where I was exposed to the ways of the metaphysical. I didn't know what the metaphysical was, but even at the age of six I remember saying to myself, *"Something is off. Something is missing. Something is causing trouble,"* and *"That's not right!"*

I think of this when I watch the film **The Matrix,** where Morpheus says to Neo: *"Let me tell you why you're here. You know something. What you know, you can't explain, but you feel it. You felt it your entire life. There's something wrong with the world. You don't know what, but it's there. Like a splinter in your mind, driving you mad."*

This unknowing eventually led me down a path of discovery where, piece by piece over a period of two decades, I uncovered the woman protector (or warrior archetype) which had been reawakening within myself. It began a journey that continues to reveal a way forward both for myself and others.

By sharing my journey and understanding thus far, it is my hope to bring awareness to the parts of ourselves that need to be acknowledged, accepted, and honored. When we do this, we are able to let go of long-running and reinforced beliefs and step into a new existence – one that all of us women deserve.

This Book is an adaptation from my master's thesis, is to propose the potential reawakening of a forgotten archetype – the Woman Protector. My own path has led me to live out this archetypal behavior, which involves both spiritual and physical, or aptly described as the 'Seen' and the 'Unseen', or the 'Physical' and the 'Non- Physical'.

Although this book was written to be read in chapter order, please treat each chapter as a separate essay and read in any order you wish. All references within this book are actual quotes, translations, or reconstructions by the author.

Hāwanawana ko mākou mau kūpuna, "Mai poina."
Our foremothers whisper, *"Do not forget."*

The Archetype of the Woman Protector

My Journey

"When the student is ready, the teacher will appear. When the student is truly ready, the teacher will disappear." —Lao Tzu

In 2002, on the advice of a dear friend, I reluctantly began life-changing studies with a very gifted quantum metaphysician. At first, my primal ego rebelled violently against the non-linear metaphysical ideas. They were so far out of my comfort zone and life experience up to that point. Denial and resistance. My existence was all I knew, which was the expected suffocating, critical, punitive, and unforgiving world had been black and white with zero gray, and with zero exceptions. It was the way I was raised. I only believed in what I could see, what was 'real', what was in physical form. The initial exposure to metaphysical principles was very much like an alien abduction where I felt I was being shown worlds that I couldn't process given my then-limited world view.

I rebelled; turned away--ran away actually. Rushed out of that first session feeling that there was an inexplicable trippy hour of my life I could never get back. I actively denigrated and even scoffed aloud at the concepts, the teachings. I paid for my session where my then 10-year-old was waiting in the lobby. I wanted out of there! But when my feet crossed the door threshold while we exited to walk to the car, the *Voice That Has No Words* said, "What if,

Michelle? What if there is some truth in these principles?" By the time we reached the car, I agreed to try it for six months.

This was the beginning of the cracking of my multi-layered armor. I gave my word to this unseen voice to try it for six months but was ready to run at any moment. Over these six months, I slowly began to open to the ideas. Sure, some I couldn't comprehend - I just began to evolve - but some made immediate sense to me once I thought and felt about each one. This was it.

I tamped down my cynicism. I was filled with both exultation and trepidation, constantly asking, "How can this be true?". What would it hurt if I explored more? What if it hurt more to not explore it? I always believed that if I was to look at those hurt parts of me that it would kill me.

It turns out that not looking at those hurt parts would be what would kill me. It took some time and constant investigation to see if what I was feeling was real; if it could be applied to my life, which honestly was a mess even if I was unable to fully admit it. I felt I was barely holding it together with an impending divorce, working two to three jobs, training as much as I could in the warrior art of Lua, and trying to be the best mother I could be. I was tired. Tired of matching the behaviors and emotions of others, not sleeping, working so hard, not having or being 'enough', being angry all the time, and not enjoying anything.

Four years before this, my warrior teacher appeared, so apparently Source (God) felt I was a ready student. I am grateful to Source for that. It was to prepare me for what lay ahead, for the work I get to do today.

This is where it began, where the spiritual white blood cells started to flood the virus in my mind, body, and spirit. The concurrent metaphysical and physical training began to deinstall and install new programming. Once started, there was no stopping the metaphysical principles from drilling into my foundation, rewiring the deeply rooted familial, societal, and institutionalized male-dominated and religious programming. I unknowingly sank into a two-and-a-half-year immersion that resulted in a death and rebirth of my spirit. Some call this a *shamanic death*.

One night when I didn't have Lua training, I lay on my stomach in my bed surrounded by books by Dr. Steven R. Hawkins – tabbing, bookmarking, note-taking, journaling when my young child knocked on the open door and entered. She tried to tell me something and I acknowledged with "Uh huh". I was not listening. "Mom, I'm going to take away your books." That quickly got my attention. "What? No, you will not!"

That laser-focused period, coupled with the pointed guidance of my metaphysician, warrior training and celibacy, led me to the revelation that nothing would ever satisfy my existence except to dedicate my life to my truth. My truth being used to the fullest during my life, why I was made this way, why I had these innate talents and gifts, and what was I supposed to do with all of this – all of this that I have denied and dimmed all this time out of fear of rejection and fear of attention? Why couldn't I just be like everyone else? Why was I so weird?

The mind splinter that had nagged me since cognition was starting to remove itself for the first time. I was truly starting to believe. I began to release control and my forcefulness on everything. As I began to live and act in that belief, I began to change, and so did everything and everyone around me. I had to say goodbye to my husband, and some beloved friends, and blood relatives.

My metaphysical journey has truly saved me. I couldn't imagine who or what I would be if Source didn't call me onto this path, a path that has and continues to demand my whole being. There is no other way for me. This path continues to strongly lead me into further study, investigation, and share and teach these principles.

"Seek the wisdom that will untie your knot. Seek the path that demands your whole being."
— **Rumi**

The Archetype of the Woman Protector

Warrior or Protector?

In converting my master's thesis into a book, it became apparent to me that the word "warrior" wasn't entirely accurate for me to convey the role of a woman warrior, ancient or today. "Warrior" and "protector" may be synonymous in some instances, while in other instances, they are not. Thus, I use protector, or warrior-protector, for this literary work as the word warrior is heavily used and possibly misused today.

Warrior is used in many different industries and for many different purposes such as fitness, energy drinks and supplements, spiritual products and services, retail products, tax services, automotive parts and products, martial arts services and products, nutrition programs, military, life coaching, and more.

Some of the urban uses of warrior are weekend warrior, yoga warrior, psychic warrior, keyboard warrior, fitness warrior, tax warrior, warrior diet conscious warrior, woman warrior (those who have survived trauma or illness), social justice warrior, road warrior, prayer warrior. These examples show how trite the term has become. It's both ubiquitous and overused to the point of cliché.

Many words are misused and overused, creating incorrect feelings or ideas about what the intended context really was. Warrior has become one of those words. Like everyone receiving a trophy today for mediocre focus, participation, attendance and efforts, the word warrior has lost its muscle. While warrior and protector will be used synonymously in this book, protector seems to be a better description of a woman warrior.

The general definition of a protector is "a person or thing that protects someone or something". The reawakened protector archetype (I propose) combines the spiritual and physical. She is both, equally. In the metaphysical sense, this is where the Divine Feminine has been feared and therefore subdued, concealed, and murdered over the centuries.

Spiritual Aspect of a Protector

"Women's Intuition" is real but has been tortured, buried, and unwelcomed. I am not telling you anything you don't already know, and some that cling to patriarchy (some women included) are sick of hearing it. While others don't even know there is a difference and do not care.

We have many spiritual women protectors who are of many different ethnicities and faiths – spiritual and religious. The spiritual aspect of a woman protector is her ability feel or know things she couldn't feel or know if she solely relied on Newtonian Physics' linear "thinkingness," or what she can see sense of physical sight; but a woman who is only spiritual is imbalanced based on this proposed archetype.

The Archetype of the Woman Protector

Physical Aspect of a Protector

Being only spiritual is imbalanced, working only in the physical is also imbalanced. I have seen some women spiritual protectors lack interest in the body and its abilities, and even their overall health. In a physical sense, many spiritual women lack consideration and provision for the basic care of their the beautiful, highly intelligent, and fragile packages in which they carry their essence. The physical body, and the health of our physical body, is directly tied to our spiritual effectiveness here on Earth.

After decades of negligent and intense behavior, I began to treat my body like a child or elderly relative that couldn't care for itself. I still work on this every day. But we need to ask ourselves: would I withhold hydration, nutrition, movement, and rest from a loved one? No! Then why do we treat our own physical body this way?

We must prepare and train consistently to meet a challenge if someone crosses our boundary of physical safety.

We must be prepared and confident in our abilities to defend ourselves and resolve to physically engage in extreme situations – for our survival.

Protector Versus Soldier

"A warrior with a cause is the most dangerous soldier of all." - Michael Scott

Some will disagree but I believe that there is a distinction between a warrior and a soldier. Soldiers are trained to do what they are told and subject to authority. They bypass their individual thinking process and conscience. Follow orders. No emotions. Only do. Ask questions later, if at all. No deviation from the orders they have been given.

In contrast, a protector utilizes intuition and wisdom, not just intellect. They appear to be of opposite intention of the soldier - engaging when they feel called to engage, how they will engage, how much they will engage, and the delivery of their engagement – if they choose to engage at all. A protector always asks why.

A woman protector's engagement is not because she is ordered to engage; it is based on personal choice and intention. Emotions mean something, but they are not the end-all be-all; more, they are merely messages on which way to go, what to do, what not to do, when, how, and how much, if at all. A protector evaluates her intention, whereas a soldier lacks the ability to set personal intention other than the mission and order she is given.

The Archetype of the Woman Protector

*A woman protector must know the why
in any decision she makes.*

In Hawaiian, **Uli'eo Koa** means protector preparedness. Living as a protector takes a lifetime commitment of purpose, discipline, and a meaningful life of service. When on the battlefield, would a protector save someone and end her life in the process? Not usually as this would be unwise. However, she would sacrifice herself in a certain circumstance. This way of life's calling may require sacrifices of all sorts, and the sacrifice of consistent comfort or convenience at times, but not to the detriment of one's own existence, unless we make that decision. The 'why' would justify this decision. Being a protector means not compromising spiritual principles and accomplishing all things with unwavering integrity.

*"Nothing that's for me, will require me to act out
of my character. Absolutely nothing."
– Unknown*

It means using what life throws at us to attain self-awareness, self-evolution, and to allow our emotions and body to inform us of what, where, when, how, and why an adjustment is needed. Through this, in our willingness and presence in the moment, our path reveals itself as we move. AS WE MOVE! Not physical movement but as we continue to do our work in the spirit and move that into physical action. All protectors have a few basic things in common areas to prepare themselves:

Mental Aspect of a Protector

In the mental sense, an unfocused mind with an unceasing internal dialogue (usually in a critical tone) will lack the necessary skills to deal with life in a peaceful way and not create collateral damage or self-sabotage. I call this relentless internal foe 'The Predator." If not aware, we will fall short of preparing to protect ourselves in life – psychically and physically. Both are important but some only focus on one or the other. We won't even discuss the financial aspect and protecting our resources!

The biggest opponent, it is said, is the one we face in the mirror.

We cannot allow temporary circumstances or people to dictate what we should focus on from moment-to-moment unless it is a life-threatening situation. Through mental clarity and discipline, we can be present in the moment, which is the only way we can even determine what a thing 'is', how or if we should focus on 'it', and if there is anything we need or should do – proactively or reactively.

One of the key attributes of a warrior is her self-discipline and perseverance.

The Archetype of the Woman Protector

Protector Energy

Some women (and even some men) remain apprehensive or scared of protector energy, synonymously known as action energy and masculine energy. It seems there is an adversity to acknowledging that we embody both Hina (feminine) and Kū (masculine) energies. While in ancient Hawaiian times there was no distinction. Today it is very helpful so that we can perceive and embody the two different expressions of these energies.

Until we feel protector energy in our body, we remain imbalanced.

Many of us women have had experiences with external masculine energy that was not pleasant and was possibly even violent. Internally when we feel it in us, we suppress it instead of acknowledging it and using it for our good. To convert this masculine energy for focus, resolve, production and to move us into action.

We destroy our physical body and mental health when we suppress our protector energy.

David Brown says, "There is always a time for warrior energy; the warrior should cut in and out of their energy as required without any shame or guilt, while recognizing their own space, their own truth and personal power." To fully welcome that power when you have the courage and strength to do what is beneficial for yourself – verbally, physically, psychically, financially, and through non-action.

We can and should use this protector energy to release any trauma or dis-ease that has been stored in our body, and to put the energy towards resolving issues or reaching a place of acceptance and completion (completion is different than closure).

Protector energy is not reserved for just fitness workouts, heated arguments, road rage, medical situations, self- or other-defense, or life-or-death situations. We can consciously choose to use protector energy in our daily lives for any use like self-discipline, focus, energy towards our goals or strategy, and for our work.

Protector energy is a part of the ego and the spirit. When healthy and understood, protector energy is helpful for our survival and to succeed in the things we wish to succeed in. Maybe we operate too much in linear energy of force, or in the wise focused protector linear and non-linear energy of power.

Operating as a protector requires us to check in with our intellect and our intuition, equally.

The Chopra Center has a website dedicated to Warrior Energy. On this website is Vedic teacher, Michelle Fondin, discusses the Third or Manipura Chakra (Solar Plexus). This area is an energetic source of personal transformational power that governs self-esteem and warrior energy. Like anything in life, each small step we take to honor our intention helps to strengthen the Third Chakra, but also helps to build healthy mental and physical habits. This, then, feeds our inner fire, called Teias in Sanskrit, and to rely on our 'gut feeling' that further attracts and draws us into action - not just waiting, hoping, and wishing for our goals and desires.

Staying in the feminine too long is not good. We need to utilize our masculine – our action energy. Moving straight into action is also not good. We need time in the feminine to strategize and plan so we know what action, and how and when to move.

To increase one's gut feeling or 'inner woman', metaphysical protectors use ceremony, ritual, and prayer to ask for clarity and assistance from the non-physical realm. These ancient practices are indispensable when addressing psychic vampires, predators, or threats. They help to resolve any known or unknown issues in the non-physical world that will eventually manifest in the physical world if not dealt with.

Dark matter (the unseen realm) makes up about 85 percent of the total matter in the universe. We must remember that the unseen 'dark matter' is not just blank nothingness of illusionary space. The word "matter" implies that it is something more concrete than an abstraction. Therefore, the entire phrase 'dark matter' is an oxymoron. Physics is leaning towards identifying dark matter as a field where information is gathered. It is now believed that this is a field of pure intelligence.

Researchers have been able to infer the existence of dark matter only from the gravitational effect it seems to have on visible matter.

Could it be that our metaphysical protector work is so powerful that it can shift things before they manifest in physical form? What if the researchers are accurate?

Protector energy uses aggression as focused intent and power. How one channels aggression determines if it will be used to produce either desired or undesired outcomes. The more we work with and in it, the more control we have over it.

We have all encountered reckless individuals with no self-control. "Blowing off steam" feels good to them but is destructive for everyone and everything around them, including themselves. We may even be this person! Maybe we were one of these women at one time or another in our lives. I was.

If we allow our aggression to go unchecked, it will cause us to fight with everyone about everything, stagnate personal development, sabotage ourselves and others, cause failures in our personal and professional relationships, manifest in fits and starts of enthusiasm – never finishing anything, and cause us to blame of all external forces for these failures and our uncontrolled responses.

We must learn how to identify, embrace, use, and master our own energy.

Externally, we must learn how to be the only master of our energy. We need to be aware when someone is attempting to manipulate or drain our energy. We also cannot be easily derailed when someone 'needs' us. I know we have nurturing DNA, but we must nurture ourselves first, and fully, on a regular basis.

The days of codependency must end for us to live a fulfilled life. There are no points or rewards for depleting ourselves for the sake of anyone. We do this by looking inward instead of blaming outward or distracting ourselves with external matters. If we suppress our aggression without an outlet, it will convert into aggression (overt and covert) that bleeds into every area of our lives. It will skew our ability to perceive and make constructive decisions, and ultimately make us physically ill. If we can successfully harness, focus, and integrate aggression energy, it will propel us into productive, thoughtful, and healthful action. We would be in the best condition of our lives!

Protector energy:

Provides a clear and definite intention of purpose. Without it, we will feel restless, overwhelmed, lost, and useless.

Compels awareness, patience, observing, studying, planning, and strategizing with progression as the intention.

Is adaptable. Even against great odds we can use our spontaneity within preparedness, ability to shift quickly, with intelligence, intuition, and calculated strategy to turn things around, or merely get and keep our plans progressing.

Traveling Prepared

We must travel through life as prepared and unburdened as possible. When we are prepared, we eliminate non-essentials that help us to keep a step ahead of any potential surprises. Protector energy is decisive and prepares for possible contingencies. We do not have the luxury of freezing, hesitating, or being in a position where we are unprepared and unable to make prompt decisions, especially in a crisis.

Protector energy is skillful, competent, powerful, and accurate. It is rooted in the discipline of self-control. We learn and know our present limits. If we feel unprepared, we develop ourselves in these areas. When we examine a situation by checking in, equally, with our intellect and intuition, we limit the fear in making decisions. We may

The Archetype of the Woman Protector

not like saying "no" to something that feels good (intuition) when it doesn't check out with the intellect. An example of this would be receiving a business contract from a company you really want to work with, but the contract does not have your best interest.

Protector energy is emotionally non-attached from fear, doubt, intimidation, manipulation, and feelings during the battle.

A protector needs room to swing her sword sometimes.

Metaphysically we swing our sword during incidents when we have to set and maintain boundaries for our well-being, and to fulfill our own hopes, dreams and contributions to the world.

The Path of the Protector

"Be wild; that is how to clear the river."
- Clarissa Pinkola Estes

As a protector - I live, train, and train others. I believe more women would choose this way of life if they knew it was available to them. But this path isn't for everyone.

We can still navigate through life in our power while being dressed as and blending well in the world as our alter-ego. It is unfortunate that we still need to do this, but it is necessary and requires moment-to-moment intuition and wisdom. Thankfully our society is changing; where women are able to speak more openly, able to advocate (carefully and strategically) for ourselves, are believed and supported more than ever, and where the Harvey Weinstein behaviors and longstanding societal destructive beliefs towards women can no longer continue behind closed doors. Yet, we know they still and will continue to do so.

We spend so much time reacting and responding to micro- and major- aggressions, we forget that we – at our very core – are creators and protectors. We forget that we are free. That we can choose freedom in the country we live in. The news shows us daily situations that are very real and, at times, threaten our physical bodies, emotional and mental wellbeing, financial condition, and our careers.

The Archetype of the Woman Protector

The world needs for us women to welcome, recognize, embrace, focus, and use protector energy to balance ourselves, and the collective energy of the planet. To powerfully reawaken by stepping into the space that has been waiting for us. For some women, this may be the first awakening into their inherent powers. While for some other women, they will not be interested in this type of freedom, accountability, and lifelong evolution.

It is my belief that protector energy is what completes a woman, as it is the fullness of how we have been made.

It is my experience that protector energy heals past trauma that has been hidden in our subconscious and stored in our physical bodies, causing dis-ease, and prohibiting us from moving forward. It is time to let our protector battle cry reverberate across the land and into the Multiverse. This doesn't mean going to the desert and screaming. While that is a beautiful physical act of clearing (and sometimes necessary), we can accomplish this right now, where we are, through our vibrational energy.

We begin to move on this path of using protector energy, communicating clearly, and no longer apologizing for the space that is rightfully ours to occupy. When we do this, peak out of our perceived smallness or dimmed existence, it will upset some friends, relatives, significant others, and co-workers.

Regardless, and sometimes directly in spite of, we need to follow the way we are strongly led.

This path is also in direct spite of our fear of attention and fear of success. We can access this courageous protector energy to work towards or even accomplish a goal, ask for a promotion, confront a friend about a boundary violation, end a romance, tighten up for financial savings, increase our physical health, or any other thing that needs our action energy (like filing your taxes and finishing your academic goals!).

Ask yourself what your life would look like, what state of health you would you be in, what your bank account would look like, and what accomplishments you would have if you decided to use protector energy more frequently and intentionally?

"I am not what happened to me. I am what I choose to become." – **Carl Gustav Jung**

Metaphysical Science

Metaphysics is the study of the very fabric of being.

Just like the interchangeability of warrior with protector, I will interchange metaphysical and spiritual throughout this book.

What is metaphysical science or metaphysics? We hear the words "metaphysical" and "metaphysics" and think of "woo-woo" *out-there* hocus pocus and UFO concepts. Images of new age people and robed gurus in meditative postures come to mind, with incense burning and music of gongs, sound bowls, and nature sounds playing in the background. Names like Moonbeam and Stardust abound. "All you have to do is this..." "You just have to..." The faux "Love & Light" and perfect social media influencers are strong in the world currently. While I like to name the faux positivity as "Love & Lies", I truly believe others are easily influenced because they seek real connection, with themselves, others, and the world. And the song "The Age of Aquarius" plays looped as a soundtrack.

Metaphysical science is the philosophical investigation of the ultimate nature of reality that exists beyond the physical world and our immediate senses.

Like the word "warrior", the word "metaphysics" has been overused and applied to so many things that have no relation to this very expansive philosophical science that was believed to have been created by the learned philosophers from Greece. When in fact, it has always been the substrate, the very foundation, of almost all ancient indigenous cultures. The "meta" is a prefix meaning "self". In translation, "metaphysical" means the science of self.

This energy, this Source, goes back to before Earth. This energy has always been in existence whether we acknowledged its existence, believed it in, or studied it. It exists today as we continue to ask the very questions our ancestors asked, "What is consciousness?" "Does the unseen world really exist?" "Who am I?" "Why am I here?" "Does the non-physical world really influence the physical world?"

Some of the basic questions within metaphysical science are:

1. Questions concerning reality as a whole;
2. Questions concerning things that must be true of absolutely everything that exists;
3. Questions concerning possibilities for existence;
4. Questions concerning fundamental aspects of contingent things; and
5. Questions concerning the nature of human beings.

Some ask how we can quantify the study of the self, metaphysics, as a legitimate scientific discipline, when the study of self is about 'beingness' which is personal to each one of us. For this reason, some will say it is pure speculation or armchair science. It is because it cannot be seen or felt in the physical realm. Well, not until it manifests from non-physical to the physical.

All philosophical branches have multiple subdivisions.

The Three Major Categories of Metaphysical Science

Metaphysics, is one of the major sections of philosophy, that breaks down to:

1. Ontological – Existence, becoming, and reality
2. Theological – Religious doctrines and their philosophical reflection
3. Atheistic – Existence of the Absolute (explicit denial of God) or the Relative (implicit denial of God but belief of an absolute power is accepted).

Metaphysical Branches

Because metaphysical science (or metaphysics) can be defined broadly, it is important to understand the different types and how the study and application of this science can better our existence. Unfortunately, there are deceivers out there profiting from our desire to self-help. We have met these individuals that have impressive lingo, pitches, presentations, with matching attire. We are barraged by their adverts for spiritual retreats and programs on social media. The metaphysical principles are packaged and marketed under the guise of self-help. The global self-help industry made $41.2 billion dollars in 2023 and is projected to grow to $81.7 billion by 2032.

After a while, we realize these teachers, healers, guides, retreats, conferences, and programs can sometimes be disingenuous. Imposters and lesser evolved teachers and guides in the spiritual or healing professions and spaces are especially dangerous. They gravely mislead those who sincerely seek, or are in the process of, spiritual transformation. In these situations, it is very important to listen to your intuition and not override it.

There are three main types of Metaphysics: Atheistic, Theological, and Ontological.

Metaphysical Atheism

Metaphysical Atheism may be either:

(a) Absolute — an explicit denial of God's existence associated with materialistic monism; or
(b) Relative — the implicit denial of God in all philosophies that, while they accept the existence of an absolute, conceive of the absolute as not possessing any of the attributes proper to God: transcendence, a personal character or unity."

Metaphysical Theology

Theological Metaphysics is becoming an area of increased study for many. This branch of metaphysics encompasses theology, holistic healing, altered consciousness, the paranormal, history, philosophy, and non-Western medicine that is applied through thought and practice.

Metaphysical Ontology

"is-ness", "being-ness", or "become-ing" Ontological Metaphysics concerns itself with the philosophical study of being, particularly with becoming, existence, reality, as well as the basic categories of 'being' and its relations.

"To be" or "not to be" is not an actual choice because you already are ('be'). You may decide to be 'this' or 'that', but the only fact is that you exist. The only question is how do we wish to exist when we are in physical form?

Regardless of preference or identification with one metaphysical branch or not, once we devote ourselves to the inquiry or investigation of self- evolution, we begin to transform through the amalgamation of the spirit to the physical body through one's mind (our powerful choice from moment-to-moment). The door to the other side, the Unseen and one's subconscious, begins to open.

The Metaphysician

The idea of a metaphysician is at least 2,000 years old. The more acceptable academic mainstream conceives a metaphysician as an expert *nature of reality* philosopher. Dr. Paul Leon Masters said, "A Metaphysical Practitioner is one who uses spiritual practices to heal not only physical conditions, but financial and emotional ones as well." Dr. Catherine Collautt states that, "A metaphysician is a doctor-healer who makes changes in the physical world through meta- physical (i.e., decidedly not 'physical') principles. As a metaphysician, Dr. Collautt works the principles of mind (and beyond) to create powerful and lasting change in peoples' lives."

When we begin to be present in both realms, we begin to realize that working in the non-physical realm is no longer negotiable. To be effective living as this proposed archetype, the Woman Protector, it requires us to work in the non-physical (metaphysical) realm, not just the physical realm.

Living solely as a physical warrior appears to be easier when we do not know any better. But as our awareness expands as we welcome working in the non-physical realm, we quickly realize living as a physical warrior is actually more difficult without the metaphysical.

When we embrace the non-physical realm, we start to recognize the parts of ourselves that we were not aware of. We eventually come into the revelation that the shifting of our perception, our decisions, and our lives are wholly dependent on the work we do in the non-physical realm.

Our work in the physical realm is directly affected by our work in the non-physical realm.

Everything starts to shift, and we begin to feel and operate in certainty, with clear resolution and unshakeable confidence.

The Archetype of the Woman Protector

The Metaphysician as a Philosopher

'Meta-' means beyond or transcending; so metaphysical means that which lies beyond, underlies, or transcends the physical realm, world, and reality.

In academic circles, "a metaphysician is a philosopher whose area of study or expertise in the study of the fundamental nature of reality and existence itself".

Physics, chemistry, and biology are the sciences that study the physical world. They are concerned with discovering and describing the properties and interactions of physical objects, which now explicitly includes energy. Metaphysics, however, is concerned with discovering and describing the principles that make these objects, properties, interactions, and principles from the non-physical.

Metaphysicians attempt to address the questions that lie beyond or behind the physical sciences. Some of the study areas include time, space, free will, meaning and value, causation, universals and particulars, polarity, coherence, substance, and appearance versus reality.

The Metaphysician as Physician

There is an older and more esoteric indigenous conception of a metaphysician outside of Western academia. This is a kind of doctor-healer who affects change in the physical world by effecting, changing, and examining what is meta-, or beyond or underlying it. The work of a metaphysician involves the psyche, the mind, the intuitive, symbolic language, quantum mechanics, and the clear understanding of the direct mind-body connection such as the psychosomatic symptoms, illnesses, and diseases. The result of metaphysical work may look like supernatural voodoo, magic, a miracle, and, on the other, like placebo or coincidence – and everything in between.

This may be because we cannot readily quantify or confirm the effect as all effects cannot be directly seen, touched, studied, or evaluated. However, the proof is how things are affected in the physical realm. It is what we call *circumstantial evidence* in law. We wake up and see it is wet outside; it is reasonable to deduce with high probability that it rained overnight while we were asleep.

Mystical Religions and Practices

Metaphysicians as mystics are as natural as physicists and mathematicians. A part of the archetype of the woman protector starts in religion and mystical practices and leads us deeply into physics. Mysticism, and its various practices, often solicit a "What the heck?!" response from individuals that have never been exposed to matters of the spirit.

The word "mystic" is misunderstood and believed to be an unqualified abstract concept, or part of The Occult today. Popular religions use of "occult" is not accurate.

Occult comes from the Latin *"occultus"* meaning clandestine, hidden, or secret.

Occult, then, is the esoteric knowledge intended for or likely understood by only a small amount of people. Whereas exoteric knowledge intended for or likely understood by the general public.

Once people hear of certain knowledge, it transitions from esoteric to exoteric. If people would dig a little deeper beyond secular religion, they would find that mystical experiences are the foundation of the world's religions and show absolute power available to all human beings.

American Theologian, Marcus J. Borg says, "In Christianity, Moses, Jesus, and Paul are central figures who experienced God. Every founder of a major world religion that we know about, for example Buddha and Muhammad, are portrayed as mystics. In Eastern Orthodoxy, worship is shaped around expected mystical experiences."

Salvation was believed to be linked with enlightenment - not atonement, holiness or performance.

The origin meaning of the ancient Greek word, "mysticism" means 'to close' or 'to conceal'. The union with 'The Absolute', 'the Infinite', or 'God' is how the mystical arts are defined, which includes a generous range of beliefs, religions, traditions, and practices.

In the early modern period, mysticism included 'out of the ordinary' experiences and states of mind, religious beliefs, ethics, myths, rites, legends, metaphysics, and ideologies.

These out of the ordinary experiences were believed to provide one with insight into the ultimate or hidden truths that create transformation.

"Broadly defined, mysticism can be found in all religious traditions, indigenous religions, folk religions, like shamanism, to organized religions like the Abrahamic faiths and Indian religions, and modern spirituality such as New Age and New Religious Movements."

Mysticism is the union with God through very personal experiences.

Marcus J. Borg says that for "People who have mystical experiences, God is not a belief, but a reality known."

Oxford University historian, Elizabeth Petroff, said in her book, "Body and Soul" that Women's Mysticism (yes, this is a real thing!) was a succession of insights and revelations about God that gradually transformed the recipient. Medieval historians believed that mystical women were experiencing the *Illuminative Stage* when they had visions that contained instructions from God. It's no wonder why our foremothers were burned at the stake.

Dr. Paul Masters said that mysticism is a much- abused word in today's world; yet it represents the highest quest for human growth and awareness. This is because mysticism has become a catch-all for everything including tealeaf reading, crystal- gazing, and UFO religions.

Practical Mysticism, through meditation and Second or Mystical Sight, is about discovering one's ultimate self-reality through connection to the deeper levels of the human mind through God.

This is important to try to understand because when we experience inexplicable experiences, we may feel like we are losing our linear faculties and may be developing mental illness. We feel fear because we cannot describe it or understand it with our linear thinking and speech or control it other than denying the experience. Not to mention talking about our experience with others!

As we begin to welcome these experiences, without having to define them or assign 'good' or 'bad' to them, we begin to not be so fearful. We are then able to be in the moment, in the experience, translate the experience, and receive the message that was meant only for us. For those of us who are seers, diviners, shamans, mystics, or even craftswomen, we must honor our spiritual lineage of sacred work as inheritors and guardians. Meaning that your ancestors may have been led similarly, if not in the same way, that you are being led now. We have our ancestors' life experiences in our DNA. How many memories of our ancestors can we access?

Well, to be born today - you have:

2 parents
4 grandparents
8 great grandparents
16 second great grandparents
32 third great grandparents
64 fourth great grandparents
128 fifth great grandparents
256 sixth great grandparents
512 seventh great grandparents
1024 eighth great grandparents
Over the past 12 generations =
4094 ancestors over 400 years.

How many experiences of the 4094 ancestors are in our DNA that affect us unconsciously? Part of our society has taught us to isolate ourselves and that we are alone. But we are not alone. Once we begin to connect with the non-physical realm, we will strongly feel this and become reliant on it to help guide us in life.

Also, part of connecting to the non-physical realm would help to restore the protector work of our ancient women. It would help to restore the energy for this generation and future generations of women protectors while balancing Mother Earth's energies. Side note: like Dark Matter and the physical body - Adam Frank of the University of Rochester believes that Mother Earth is a form of intelligence that is significantly influenced by the vast mycorrhizal fungi underground networks that evidences a collective cognition and action on a global scale.

Connecting to the intelligent non-physical realm helps us to resume the very work that our foremothers (and forefathers) were doing before they laid down their swords. Many indigenous cultures revered and lived in unison with nature, which was their only religion; ever aware of what the soil, mountains, rivers, oceans, wind, sky, stars, weather, and animals needed and were saying.

For most indigenous cultures, a polytheistic belief structure governed their world. There was no feared chaos because as mystics, they believed (like all mystics), that their world was coherent, consolidated, and organized around unifying patterns. It was the honorable reverence they had, as a collective, for all the elements that made up nature. By today's standard, this belief and practice would be considered mysticism.

While a protector's weaponry, response, and delivery has changed in today's world to injustice, the battle has not.

The Metaphysical Protector

Who is the protector when she is not protecting?
Who is the warrior when she is not at war?

The Buddha is alleged to have said, "Rare it is in the universe to be born into a human lifetime; rarer still is it to hear of the dharma (fulfillment of one's duty); rare still is it to accept the teachings; rarer still is it to act on the teachings; and even rarer still is it to realize the truth of the teachings".

Dr. David R. Hawkins said that to hear the teachings of enlightenment is already the rarest of gifts and that "Anyone who has ever heard of enlightenment will never be satisfied with anything else."

Spiritual protectors (metaphysicians) have an expanded awareness, are patient, courageous, disciplined, and live a life of service coined as love in action (even when it is 'tough love'). A metaphysical protector makes a lifetime commitment to purpose, discipline, and a meaningful life of service that requires sacrifices of comfort or convenience at one time or another.

Being a metaphysical protector means making a lifetime commitment to embrace discipline, study, and long intense training to live a purposeful, meaningful life of service.

Our civilized Western Society loves to title and label everything. We see this a lot in the field of psychology.

The Archetype of the Woman Protector

There are far more diagnoses now than when I studied psychology in the mid-1990's. The spiritual protector, the metaphysical protector, and metaphysicians are synonymous as they all deal in the unseen world of what psychoanalyst Carl Jung called the "Collective Unconscious". Dr. David R. Hawkins calls this realm the "Collective Consciousness" - the Radiant Divinity that is simultaneously 'within' and 'without', and simultaneously neither, yet both". Today, this Collective Consciousness is referred to by other names such as God, Goddess, Spirit, Source, Divinity, Mother, Father, Great Spirit, and The Universe.

But just as a tree in English is a called *kumulā'au* in Hawaiian, *boom* in Dutch, *arbre* in French, this creative being or force ('It') is called Magic by witches, Prayer by religious people, Manifestation or Goddess by spiritual people, the Placebo Effect by Atheists, the Universe by philosophers, and Quantum Physics by scientists. Everyone seems to differ in what It is called, but no one is denying Its' existence.

A metaphysical protector understands that, regardless of what name is given, she works in the non-physical realm as much as she does in the physical realm.

What we do (content) is directly related to who we are (context).

Metaphysical protectors rely on their intuition, which we believe is one's direct connection to Source, and know that they are the product of their thoughts. Adam Brady says that being a "spiritual warrior implies that one combats the most insidious and universal enemy – ignorance. This ignorance of the true nature of the world invokes countless forms of suffering is known as *Avidya* in Sanskrit."

"You are 90% subconscious in the way you handle life. Everything you do is accomplished by the work of the subconscious. The interaction between the conscious mind (volition) and the subconscious mind (the Law of Action) explains and determines your experience."

The Mystics

"The Soul has been given its own ears to hear things Mind does not understand." **– Rumi**

Pre-colonial "ways-of-knowing-in-being" was indigenous philosophy *and* science. Therefore, it is easy to conclude that all indigenous cultures were the first metaphysicians or the 'first metaphysics'. Today in academia, indigenous metaphysics is thought to be completely invisible, reduced to something unphilosophical like a form of ceremony and mystical garnish without a credible or theoretical base with a linear explanation.

The post-colonial term, metaphysics, is a derivative of the earlier term Mysticism. When philosophers like

The Archetype of the Woman Protector

Socrates and Aristotle began to dig deeper and ask questions like, "Why do I exist?", "Does existence exist outside of the Mind?", "What is the meaning of [my] life?", "What is real?", the academic study of the known and unknown was officially born. Aristotle, referred to metaphysical science as the "First Philosophy", or sometimes "wisdom", which is the foundation for all philosophy.

These concepts were originally published by Aristole's editor after his treatises on science because they didn't fit into that category. In the Hawaiian culture, *'pohi'* means dark while *'hihi'* means entangle, spread, snare, web, intermingle. *Pohihihi* could then be defined as the obscure, entangled, mysterious, intricate, and confusing. It is the term I use for the required metaphysical studies that are within the warrior curricula in my system, *Nā Koa* (the Warriors) and *Pā Lua 'o Manu* (School of Lua, Manu lineage).

Today metaphysical science has expanded, is more encompassing, involving the study and workings of the indigenous peoples, nature of reality, potentiality, actuality, alchemy, mind, matter, space, time, free will, Goddess, God, Spirit, Great Spirit, Source, Divinity, Divine, Allness, Absolute, Infinite, Father, or Mother, identity, change, and more.

My research has revealed that in ancient times, there was not a single woman protector who was not also a mystic.

The Physical Protector

"Be wild; that is how to clear the river."
— Clarissa Pinkola Estes

It is an erroneous to think that it was solely men, in ancient times, that were the only ones who engaged in war and protection. The vision of a knight on a charging horse, gripping his sword, while the women and children screamed, ran, and cowered. The vision of heavily armed men has become so associated with the art of war that, despite the evidence throughout history of many revered female fighters, strategists and leaders, the association between women and war is still mostly seen as somewhat of a novelty or myth that is exacerbated by today's mainstream media. It is consistently projected only as certain concepts or aspects of images of a woman warrior-protector. Despite being an exception here and there, the depictions are usually broad, usually mythical, sometimes comical, and mostly always sexual. Our warrior foremothers are presented as mythic fictional characters in supernatural fairytales. They lack depth and/or understanding of what and who ancient women warrior-protectors were.

The Archetype of the Woman Protector

Despite the evidence throughout history of revered women warriors, fighters, strategists, and trusted leaders, women are still seen as novel or fictional participants, if at all. This perception is exasperated by today's patriarchal media. Marvel Comics has heroines in their 20's to the age of 52 with Cate Blanchett - recently killing it in the role of Hela in Ragnarök. As you would expect, video gamers are upset that female warriors and soldiers are being added to video games. They believe that the addition of these 'fictional' characters are to appease feminists. In the mainstream, the concept of women warrior-protectors is easy to question based on the erroneous depictions and lack of accurate accounts for hundreds and thousands of years. Our foremothers are presented as mythic fictional characters in supernatural fairytales because their existence couldn't possibly be real.

As an example, a skeleton discovered in 1880 long assumed to be male until 2017 when DNA evidence provided it was actually that of a woman. This woman warrior-protector of Birka (Sweden) died with a crowded grave buried alongside goods that included "a sword, an axe, a spear, armor- piercing arrows, a battle knife, two shields, two horses, one mare and one stallion; thus, the complete equipment of a professional warrior, as well as a full set of gaming pieces, which indicates knowledge of tactics and strategy, stressing the buried individual's role as a high-ranking officer."

DNA analysis of the skeleton confirmed that the individual was a woman older than 30 years old, who stood somewhere around 5 feet 6 inches tall with types of skeletal signals of a warrior. Legends of ferocious female warrior-protectors appear in Scandinavian lore and poetry from the Middle Ages, but the existence of warrior women and Viking culture has consistently been challenged in official histories, with women often relegated to non- combatant roles. In medieval sources, women usually play a supporting role to the story's male hero. This has also been the popular woman warrior version told by male warrior elders in Hawai'i for the last two hundred years. Evidence is consistently being discovered to state otherwise.

These DNA findings have been highly disputed. The 'archaeology' has not changed. The only thing that has changed is our knowledge that it's a woman and not a man.

If the word warrior is overused, then "woman warrior" is underused or terribly misused. Its use almost always connotes a negative of some sort and this is a problem. The issue is our urban use of "warrior" for everything and anything. It minimizes its deeper meaning.

Merlin Stone said in her book *When God Was a Woman* that "The female divinity, revered as warrior or hunter, courageous soldier, or agile markswoman, was sometimes described as possessing the most curiously masculine attributes, the implications being that her

The Archetype of the Woman Protector

strength and valor made her something of a freak or physiological abnormality."

Honestly, all women are warrior-protectors to me. We have all had to live in a society where we have to navigate so carefully, whether that is in corporate America, in our family and cultural dynamics, in our relationships, and to avoid drawing less than safe attention from strangers when we are in public.

We have been told that it is bad to 'fight back' or to show aggression (even if really it's just assertiveness). In self-defense against violence, we have been told to be quiet, not make a scene, and to "be a good girl". We have more instances than not where a woman rightfully protected herself only to later be disbelieved, gaslighted, blackballed, and/or even blamed for the entire incident as if she provoked it, even by other women. The deeply ingrained lifelong programming by traditional morality, reinforced by society and sometimes those close to us, has kept us from moving forward powerfully and elegantly in the truth of who we are and what we have always been.

It is said that woman is the only living thing that has relationship with her only nature predator – man. A recent viral meme, viewed over 17 million times, asked women if they would rather encounter a man or a bear if they were alone in the woods. As you guessed, bear was the popular choice – seven women choosing a bear and one woman choosing a man. Hard and fast statistics show that we have a 1 in 2.1 million chance of getting mauled by a bear versus women's chance of getting raped is 1 in 6.

Among other reasons, according to Facebook and Reddit posts, why women say they would choose a bear and a man:

"No one would question me about what I was wearing if the bear attacked me."

"If I survive the bear attack, I will not have to see the bear at family reunions."

"A bear would not film it and send it to his friends."

"No one will question if the bear attack really happened."

"The bear will either kill me or leave me alone, there are not 400 other horrible ways a bear can hurt me."

Hysterically, one woman said, "To all the men feeling attacked right now... maybe you should try smiling."

In an authentic effort to connect to access the power that fueled our foremothers, sometimes through ancestral DNA memory, we talk a lot about being 'warriors' and 'protectors'. Some engage in power generated breathing exercises and chants. While others hold a short staff at an event, take pictures in what they think is warrior attire, and talk tough about defending and believing that they have the courage and tools to act, if and when it is ever time. While this is a good start, it is false confidence and does not prepare us as physical and spiritual warrior-protectors. Our power comes from who we are, not what we can physically generate. Holding a staff and attempting to generate force is of the physical realm. It is not accessing the non-physical realm and its non-linear power which is our true essence.

In this way, we cannot fake it till we make it. We either are or are not.

It's no wonder, then, in an effort to connect to the same power (Source) that empowered our protector foremothers, sometimes through ancestral memory that is stored within our DNA, we talk about being warriors and protectors without understanding what that really means.

The women we see holding a short staff or bo (like a walking stick) at an event, taking pictures in what they believe to be warrior-protector attire, and talk tough about self-defense and protection, and to act. This is perhaps a good start but does not make us prepared to feel, harness, and operate effectively in our protector energy. It isn't about emulating what we *think* our warrior foremothers were. It is about feeling *who* and *what* they were. It is about deeply feeling *who* and *what* we are, in us. For us it is accessing that same energy while we are in the process of "becoming" to eventually arrive at effortlessly "being" while we are operating in our protector energy. This energy is waiting to flow through our physical bodies, not merely be a mental concept and non-substantive belief.

This mixture of balanced qualities are the timeless spiritual virtues exemplified in and through the time-bound physical realm — through you.

A warrior should never save others from their own wars as it is part of their path. A protector understands that there is much more to engagement and her choices than merely the glory of the ego. Her goal is to protect, and she has prepared herself to do so. If a protector responds, she is connected to the intuitive and dedicates herself to exude great wisdom, skill, and timing. In contrast to a soldier, who only engages when ordered in the wars of other people; while a protector engages when it is on her own terms and when it is her war alone.

Many of us today, male and female, lack warrior energy. I can see why most avoid warrior energy as it is a very powerful and intense fire energy. Maybe we have never internally experienced it, or maybe we have, and it scared or harmed us. Maybe we have externally experienced it, but most likely repeatedly by unhealthy people. Because of this we vow to not want any part of it. Of course, masculine (action) energy should be immediately accessed while in a violent or life-threatening situation. But it is an energy that should be accessed daily for our betterment as it provides balance, healing, and prepares us.

Men and women balance their energies and even learn differently. There is growing research that men and women

The Archetype of the Woman Protector

are fundamentally and biologically different in ways that affect behavior — and that the difference favors women. I believe the myth that there is no such fundamental difference not only flies in the face of the facts of evolution, genetics, hormones, brain science, psychology, and cross-cultural studies, but it hurts the equality cause for both men and women. It depends on what space we are talking about.

I spoke with one of few remaining martial masters and elders of the only native warrior art, *Ku'ialua* (modernly known as "Lua") of Hawai'i. He said that training in Lua for men is, in this order - techniques, conditioning, and then the mind. Through the training of a brutal joint dislocation combat art, a man gained conditioning, and then control of his mind.

As a woman teacher of the modern Lua, in contrast, I have found that women learn in this order: mind, conditioning, then techniques. When men get frustrated, they switch into hyper focus. When women get frustrated during their training they disconnect, succumb to the critical internal dialogue, and quit.

In my teaching experience, I agree that there are gender differences. How could there not be? I have seen that it is a 180-degree difference in the way men ready their body for more power than how women ready their body. Men use their laser focus and move into action, whereas women seem to have internal dialogue of whether they can do it, want to do, or don't want to hurt anyone even if someone wants to hurt them. To know this helps us learn and operate with more understanding and that one approach is not better than the other, just different.

Instead of learning in a content focused way like men do, women learn in the context focused way, asking "Why?" before they decide to learn. The action of a woman protector is thoughtful, with intent, and complete. She uses her intent and will to shape her life. Using her metaphysical connection to the Divine, her "women's intuition", to strongly guide her using feminine energy and masculine energy.

An example of this is *Scáthach*, a real-life (not mythical) Scottish warrior queen, educator of warriors, weapons maker, metaphysician, seer, and priestess. It is said that *Scáthach*, who lived sometime in the centuries on either side of 200 BC, was the only one during this time that was the warrior trainer of men. No one defied her leadership out of fear of her spiritual power and physical proficiency. After all, she was their teacher.

Mystical women were and are simultaneously connected with the physical world and the spiritual world.

Today, most of us don't know this or have chosen not to believe this. Through these mystical experiences, we are transformed. Through our transformation, we transform the world. I encourage you to be courageous and transform into a modern-day protector. I have and I can no longer choose to live any other way.

We need to know – deeply know – that a physical altercation is not over until it is over. In a physical altercation, we resolve, with our life, to never give up even if we are hurt, and feel and smell warm blood. We may feel like we are losing – but it is not over until it is over! Hopefully with you ultimately removing yourself (and your loved ones) to a safe place. The mental grit of a protector is needed at all times – not only when we are a weekend warrior of an activity - and this can only be developed through physical contact and training.

Consistent training helps us to know what we are capable of by using the tools and movements we have worked on, or even mastered. We must train so that our nervous system does not go into a momentary shock or freeze when we are touched in ways we have never been touched before, and this touch will most likely be with surprise and force.

To prepare, mentally and physically, for the possibility of more than one attacker, and in different environments such as in your car, a store, at your workplace, while pumping gas, in your bedroom, while traveling on a plane, and attacked with a weapon. Physical training is perishable. The skills you learn, and the fitness required to survive a physical event, must be dedicated to and regularly trained in.

What movements in your workout will assist you in protecting yourself and others?

Instead of working out or going for a walk just for movement, set your intention to increase your abilities to protect. Do you know what it feels like to hit the floor? Do you know how to fall from certain angles to minimize the initial contact to your body? If you are shoved and forcefully hit the ground, does your current fitness level allow you to roll and reasonably get off the floor? If not, do you know how to protect yourself while you are on the ground? Does the fitness of your core allow you to maneuver and block from incoming force while on the floor?

What about being shoved against the wall. Do you know what that feels like? Do you know how to deflect the initial impact throughout your entire body? Do you know how to use that initial impact by bouncing off the wall?

Does your current level of balance allow you to stay upright and not be knocked down to the ground? Do you know how to warrior walk to keep your power in the feminine regeneration to use for protection? Do you know how to snap kick a charging dog?

Do you know what it feels like to be hit in all parts of your body with increased amounts of force? This is important otherwise you will freeze during a physical altercation. That freeze will impact the outcome. Do you know what it feels like to hit something or someone? If not, the reverberation of the energy will also make your body freeze when it should respond.

There is no time to process during a physical incident. This must be done regularly in our preparedness training, not during an incident. We work with what we have. Our mind may be strong and resolved that we will survive whatever comes our way. But our body should match this resolve through its physical training for our ultimate preparedness for when we must protect.

"If you think you can survive a violent event without violence, you are already dead."
– Michelle Manu

Archetypal Energy

We all see a lot of writings in our society that have messages - overt and covert – concerning gender superiority. I, too, have societal programming that doesn't allow me to fully see the intended or implied messages. In these instances, I always rewrite he or him to she or her. This always gives me the full unbiased picture of how prevalent it is in our society. In this example, I changed the "she" to "he":

"When choosing a man who works, you have to accept that he can't handle the house.

"If you have chosen a man who can take care of you and fully manage your household, you have to accept that he is not earning money.

"If you choose an obedient man, you must accept that he depends on you and you must ensure his life.

"If you decide to be with a strong man, you have to accept that he is tough, and he has his own opinion.

"If you choose a beautiful man, then you will have to accept big expenses.

"If you decide to be with a successful man, you must understand that he has character and has his own goals and ambitions."

When I read this with "she" throughout, it isn't as shocking, as we are somehow used to this messaging. But when "he" was inserted, I quickly saw how demeaning this writing was.

Discussing the archetypes in gender really isn't the focus of this book.

The focus is taking who we know women to be and ascribing those energetic and physical qualities to archetypes that are presented to us as male.

We should no longer discuss metaphysical truths as merely intellectual masculine concepts of 'action' and

The Archetype of the Woman Protector

'doing' as they are also rooted in the intuitive feminine energy of 'being' and 'feeling'. Is it possible they co-exist and need one another to exist? I believe so! Equal but opposite. In physics, this is proven to not merely be a lofty concept.

An example of this would be how "*Ha*" (hah) in the Hawaiian culture has been historically presented as masculine for hundreds of years. *Ha* is The Breath or Breath of Life. But what happened to "*Hi*" (hee) the feminine, the inhale of breath where the mana (power) is actually generated? Without the *Hi* there would be no *Ha*. Try breathing in and not breathing out, or vice versa.

Are we adjusting, with equal consideration, using the introspective and strategic feminine before we convert the feminine into active kinetic masculine? We do not just get in the car and drive. We calculate where we are going then move into purposeful action. Could we apply this belief to our daily lives and our seasonal, 1-year, and 5-year plans?

As we seek this balanced and whole way of being, a woman protector also understands that her current level of consciousness (awareness) is the total sum of her life experiences, stored pain, and consistent thoughts. If we were to erase all the things we wish to erase, we would also be erasing all the wisdom we learned from each of those experiences. We would erase who we are.

As protectors, we must understand that our consciousness at each moment is the law that defines, perceives, and executes our moods, beliefs, intentions, and convictions. We must be connected to, and aligned with, our shadow self and truth. We must understand that self-inventory must be looked at every moment, to ask questions and have communication with ourselves (the feminine), and release what we can – things that are not ours.

When we do our work as protectors, we have to determine what belongs to us and what belongs to others. Working in the energetic non-physical realm births physical things, such as ailments and illnesses that manifest in the body. It also births alignment, peace, health, abundance, and tremendous opportunities.

The protector knows that her life is a product of her belief systems, intentions, and thoughts. They make up our level of consciousness, our energetic field – our essence. This energetic field is our context from which all content is birthed. But somewhere along the way of surviving and fulfilling our pragmatic physical obligations, some of us have forgotten the personal energetic power we store and that is ready for our use.

Maybe, like all protectors, this personal power has always been presented as a myth to us and reinforced by society that it belongs to men. Through our busyness in the physical realm, we continue to lose connection with Source and those that walk with us and assist us in the non-physical realm. Academia and careers promote only physical self-study as part of psychology, psychoanalysis, behaviorism, humanism, and others. But the substrate, the core of these studies, is quantum metaphysical – the non-physical.

Author Sanjay Singh says that Carl Gustav Jung's "Analytical Psychology" was "... chiefly concerned with the psyche itself, leaving out body and spirit in his research." He believed that the psychic experience is the only immediate experience and that the body is as metaphysical as the spirit". If Dr. Jung believed that the body was just as metaphysical as the spirit, why didn't he also study the body? To me, I cannot see how one can be separated from the other, especially when discussing energy and how they directly affect one another.

In fact, I believe the body is the messenger of energy.

"The mind does not, like many assume, live in the brain, the mind lives in the body. The so-called Body-Mind. Any conflict that exists in our reality, in our life and in our relationships, also exists in the body - as facial tension." -
David Manning

While we discuss archetypes, we will attempt to classify the energy and correlating qualities that each archetype seeks to represent. Until recently, most archetypes have been presented to us as being male. Even the female archetypes discussed today in public are still tied to patriarchal definitions of what the feminine should or should not be. Some are the lover, queen, huntress, maiden, crone, mother and more recently the girl boss, diva, and baddie. Oh, please. Stop!

The male archetypes that will be addressed are the Warrior, Magician, and Sage.

Rewriting Archetypes

Male Archetypes

Warrior Archetype

The Male Warrior Archetype is described as a creative destroyer, destroying only to make room for something more constructive. The Warrior is emotionally detached during a mission, disciplined, minimalist, decisive, adaptable, and had a purpose.

Psychoanalyst, Dr. Carl Jung, states that the Male Warrior (or Hero) Archetype is related solely to male virility, eroticism, power, and physical strength. The Warrior maintains composure and never panics; possesses a gift for quick but rational thinking with good instincts; can be obsessive by nature and need to prepare for battle; chooses conflict as a means of solving problems, escalating problems when it was not necessary; and can rage and have lack of control of their emotions.

The Archetype of the Woman Protector

Magician Archetype

The Male Magician Archetype is the bearer of ancient and new knowledge and possesses great power to create and channel power for the good of all. In ancient times, kings would always have a wizard, magician, or seer by his side to serve as the king's strategist and to use the magician's discernment. This archetype can also be synonymous with the Sage Archetype (below), Seer, Knower, Shaman, Wizard or Alchemist. Think of Gandalf in *Lord of the Rings*, or Albus Dumbledore in *Harry Potter*, or Yoda in *Star Wars*.

Sage Archetype

The Male Sage, through objectiveness, is always in search of the uncomfortable truth. With inward goals, the Sage is a custodian of wisdom and is a great adviser. He is typically depicted as an older wise man. Think of Morpheus in *The Matrix*, and again Gandalf, Dumbledore, and Yoda. This archetype is a wise and profound philosopher that seeks truth, no matter how uncomfortable it may get in that pursuit. Sages are truth seekers and great advisers.

Female Archetypes

Warrior Archetype - Female

Let us rewrite the male warrior archetype to read, "The Warrior Archetype is related to female virility, eroticism, power, and physical strength". Better yet, let us remove the gender association altogether to read, "The Warrior Archetype is related to virility, eroticism, power, and physical strength."

In removing gender, we can see how this would change if it were a woman! Personally, I do not believe that living as a woman protector, today or in ancient times, is or ever was solely related to female virility, eroticism, power, and physical strength.

In contrast, the woman protector archetype is also creative destroyer, destroying those who threaten what is loved, whether it be land, any living thing, or beloved place or item. The woman protector aligns with the purpose of all warrior foremothers who were protectors and mystical. The woman warrior was not emotionally detached and was connected with Source, her guardians, and ancestors during the entire mission; was disciplined, minimalist, decisive, adaptable, and had a purpose.

Magician Archetype - Female

I see the woman magician archetype very different than the male magician archetype. While the bearer of ancient and modern knowledge from the non-physical realm, these women had tremendous power and assistance from unseen energies to create and channel power for good or evil. I also see that these women may have preferred to

The Archetype of the Woman Protector

be alone most of the time, not serving a king and the king's wants. I believe the goal of a woman magician was to protect, serve up punishment, and to cause healing or harm. I believe they were seers, knowers, priestesses, and alchemists but operated as they pleased.

Sage Archetype - Female

The woman sage archetype also searches for truth and a bearer of wisdom. Also, a great advisor, I don't believe women sages were older. One's connection with Source dictates one's wisdom of the non-physical realm – not someone's chronological age. Like the magician, this archetype is self-governing and self-acting.

The Woman Protector

Let's take the three male archetypes – the Warrior, Sage, and Magician - combine them, make them feminine, add the Body, add the Spirit, and add God-Intuitive. This is my proposed archetype that expands on what Jung psychologically focused (the Mind) by incorporating the body and spirit.

If we combine the intellect (reason), intuitive (spirit), and warrior (physical) aspects, this is what I believe to be a woman protector.

Women protectors are warriors with non- physical and physical abilities. Protectors comprehend and readily discern the energies they are exposed to. The energies they feel and become aware of are of their own individual energetic body, the energy of the energetic bodies in their immediate surroundings, the energetic body of the Collective Consciousness, planetary energy, energy of the Multiverse, and the energetic body of Source (Divinity or Allness). They know that their work changes things, and raises and offsets the level of the Collective Consciousness of all of humankind. Protectors understand that they live in an ever- evolving existence and are sensitive to the energy shifts. They understand that their connection to Source is within each breath, through their choice.

A protector is ever adjusting to balance herself in timeless spiritual and timebound physical realms.

While working for the betterment of all living things, a protector lives a fulfilled existence - one that is in the present, thoughtful, empowered, and free. She has accepted who she has been, who she is now, and embraces all the experiences that will shape who she will become. She knows, without a doubt, that she is a manifestor – directly affecting the physical realm through her work in the metaphysical realm. If called to, she is open to helping others in both the physical and non- physical.

A protector uses prayer, rituals, spiritual writings, movement, and other practices to connect with Source. A protector uses martial arts, yoga, and other movements to commune with Source, to relieve the body from stored emotions and trauma, for healing, self-evolution, and for information.

The Archetype of the Woman Protector

We cannot discuss these truths as merely intellectual linear concepts anymore.

Dr. Hawkins spoke about the difference "know about," "knowing," and "knowingness." We may "know about" concepts on the surface. We may also have a "knowing" about concepts just beyond the surface level. And we eventually arrive at the irrefutable and non-negotiable "knowingness" at our core. **This is to be identified, absorbed, felt deeply, and placed into active action in our daily lives.** If we can do this, we realize that there is no other state of being that is as fulfilling.

"We were put here on earth to act as agents of the Infinite, to bring into existence that which is not yet, but which will be, through us." – Steven Pressfield

To honor Source, and to be fully effective in the matters that Source has entrusted to us, it is our duty to become as aware as possible this lifetime. I feel that if we could embrace and enact our fully awakened life - through body, mind, and spirit - we would become effective and used for the greater good for all of humankind. Through this way of life, we truly exemplify the power of our thoughts through connection with Source, forming one's belief system through Source, that governs one's life through one's subconscious mind. All while having the ability to physically protect and kick some booty.

Feminine and Masculine Energies

We are healing and transforming so we can be wise grandmothers and divine women who get to powerfully live outside the cycle that has been - to powerfully model these awakened parts of ourselves. And as we begin to embrace our tendencies and our gifts, as we develop our talents, we begin to fracture the dysfunctional and destructive cycle, and reawaken and welcome the dormant protector within. Or, maybe our protector proficiencies need to be honed a bit more.

To live as a protector means we are living in the physical realm while equally operating in the non-physical realm.

We do this by using our intellect (physical) and intuitive (non-physical). Protector energy is not just action or masculine energy. Without the feminine potential energy, there would be no masculine explosive energy.

As we've discussed, the feminine and masculine are objectively opposite and equal energy expressions. Siding with one energy over the other is equivalent to believing the pervasive lie that men are superior to women. We are told that, by nature, men are genetically predisposed to be physically stronger in every way but that women have a higher pain tolerance.

During the time of the COVID-19 pandemic, it seems even biology contradicted this belief. In 2020, doctors said that hospitalized men with COVID-19 were 75% more likely to die than women hospitalized with the respiratory disease. It is believed that the innate immune response tends to be stronger in women and that infected women may have more luck keeping their viral loads low.

Some believe that women are superior to men in many ways, thus why matriarchal societies were burned and in oppression going back twelve millennia. Our world is different now, so we do not know if matriarchy was truly any less violent or harmonious. We do know that men and women are fundamentally and biologically different in ways that affect behavior — and that these differences favor women, not men.

I believe that gender superiority not only flies in the face of the facts of evolution, genetics, hormones, brain science, psychology, and cross- cultural studies, but it hurts patriarchy and healthy feminism. There is absolutely no benefit from believing that one gender is superior to the other. To say that women are equal to men would be holding women back.

Believing a certain gender is superior to the other only separates us more and promotes the pervasive inequality between the genders. Science has proven that opposite energies are like magnets. When we experience an imbalance within the essence of our male and female energies, the lack of polarity in disastrous producing harmful effects in our physical body, our mental body, and in our society to be repeated for generations to come.

Marti Angel, a health expert and coach says, "When a person is stuck on the right, the male manic side, then the body becomes wiry and thin and heart attacks become prevalent. When stuck on the left, the female depressive side, the person becomes lethargic and fat and easily depressed."

Nancy Qualls-Corbett says that "When the Divine Feminine, the Goddess, is no longer revered, social and psychic structures become over mechanized, over politicized, over militarized. Thinking, judgment, and rationality become the ruling factors. The needs for relatedness, feeling, caring, or attending to nature go unheeded. There is no balance, no harmony, neither within oneself nor in the external world. With this disregard of the archetypal image so related to passionate love, a splitting off of values, a one-sidedness, occurs in the psyche. As a result, we are sadly crippled in our search for wholeness and health."

Within the pseudoscience of Alchemy, Jim Self states that "Masculine energy is made up of straight lines and angles. Feminine energy is made up of curves and swirls. The masculine energy holds about 40 points of energy and has no swirls or curls. The feminine energy holds about 140 points of energy and has no straight angles or lines.

The Archetype of the Woman Protector

Feminine energy is very expansive, very creative, and very fluid. Feminine energy can do 25 things at one time while it swirls and curves. Masculine energy says, "Straight line, go down a straight line."

Mr. Self continues to say that without the other, the masculine or feminine energies are incomplete, not nurtured or appreciated, unsupported, not focused, scattered and unstable and without purpose. "Female energy without masculine energy is not whole. Masculine energy without female energy is not whole."

In psychology, it is currently taught that masculine energy is concerned with "doing," whereas feminine energy is concerned with "being" or "feeling."

A renowned Jungian professor, Dr. Clarissa Pinkola Estés, in her book, "Women Who Run with the Wolves," says that when a woman consciously recognizes and holds her dual aspect of her psyche together, as a unit, she is tremendously powerful. Both need to be fed equally and neither side should be neglected, but that power of the two is very strong. Dr. Estés states that the end of women's psychological, emotional, and spiritual powers comes from separating them [masculine and feminine] from one another and pretending one or the other does not exist.

This is the equivalent to the Cherokee story of two wolves - the White Wolf versus the Black Wolf in that there is a war going on inside of us. If we feed both 'wolves', both the light and shadow sides of ourselves win. There are good and bad aspects to both sides.

"You see, the white wolf needs the black wolf at his side. To feed only one would starve the other and they would become uncontrollable. To feed and care for both means they will serve you well and do nothing that is not a part of something greater, something good, something of life. Feed them both and there will be no more internal struggle for your attention. And when there is no battle inside, you can listen to the voices of deeper knowing that will guide you in choosing what is right in every circumstance. Peace is the Cherokee mission in life. A man or a woman who has peace inside has everything. A man or a woman who is pulled apart by the war inside him or her has nothing. How you choose to interact with the opposing forces within you will determine your life. Starve one or the other or guide them both."

Dr. Paul Leon Masters said the reality of oneness with Source must be greater in your mind than any conditioned limitations that society has placed on your sense of selfhood. Setting aside all gender societal conditioning, do we really feel like we can choose our selfhood, or do we maneuver powerfully, elegantly, and as effectively as we can until the world transforms? Could it be that we cause the world to transform as we maneuver powerfully and elegantly? How can it not?! A good place to start is to

The Archetype of the Woman Protector

evaluate and dismantle all polarizing societal programming.

Here are examples of the masculine and feminine energy qualities:

Masculine Aggressive Analytical Assertive Busy Concrete Controlling Doing Hard Impatient Left Brain Logical Organizing Rushing Striving Trusting

Feminine Surrender Intuitive Receptive Calm Abstract Allowing Being Soft Patient Right Brain Creative Synthesizing Nurturing Tranquil Receiving

When we examine the above ways of being, it is clear that we have been taught to choose one or the other. But what if we could choose a middle point? We could do this by taking a thought, situation, or goal into our minds and try to balance it by asking if we are checking in with both our intuition (feminine) and intellect (masculine). Dr. David Hawkins teaches on Duality and Non-Duality. Could it be that existence is really a trinity – three parts – the middle being *lohaki*, the Hawaiian word for harmony.

As an example, let's use a situation where a loved one is in the cycle of consistently using you for her gain. Taking this situation and applying the following, what is the healthy middle ground response?

*Do you get aggressive because you are fed up? Do you surrender because you just do not wish to deal with it?

Or, what is the middle ground between these two? You decide and then ask yourself if your decision conditions this behavior to happen again in the future and does this honor your loved one in truth and love? Do your actions stop your loved one from learning her lesson?

*Do you only use your intellect, or do you also consider your intuition? Does it make sense and how do you feel about it? What does your inner woman say without you trying to suppress or downplay your gut feeling? More, what does your inner woman say when you do not consider the blowback response to your decision? Does this anticipated blowback change what actions your inner woman would take?

*Would you choose to be assertive while being receptive? Can you only be assertive and receptive without healthy boundaries while being fueled by emotions (when pushed too far)?

*Do you respond in mania or apathy? Would you choose to remain focused on problem solving while staying neutral?

*Do you have to participate at all?

*What should you do and what should you allow to just be without inserting yourself into someone else's situation?

The Archetype of the Woman Protector

It is important to recognize and acknowledge that we do not have to rush into someone else's expectations that their issue is now ours and with a sense of urgency and immediate response. What if we nurtured the pause before giving a response? We deserve the time to process and come to our own truth in each situation, especially when it is our situation. What if we converted "have to" responses to "I choose to" (if you make that decision)? Like everything in Divinity, it is about fair energetic exchanges. We should receive or release, too, and not have to earn a relationship through our performance, rescues, and perceived worthiness, closeness, support, and love.

In the modern Hawaiian culture, there is much discussion about *Kū* (the masculine) and *Hina* (the feminine). Practitioners of Lua (combat warrior art), *Lualomi* (warrior massage), *Hula* (dance), and *Pohihihi* (metaphysical) reference these essential interrelated energies in these practices of warriorism, protecting, and healing – spiritual, physical, and in movement. Wave riders also make direct analogies to the *nalu* (wave) that embodies and literally shows both energies take form in the *moana* (ocean).

"In Ancient Chinese philosophy, *Yin* and *Yang* ("dark-bright" "negative-positive") is a concept of Dualism, describing how seemingly opposite or contrary forces are complementary, interconnected, and interdependent in the natural world, and how they may give rise to each other as they interrelate to one another. In Chinese cosmology, the Universe creates itself out of a primary chaos of material energy, organized into the cycles of *Yin* and *Yang* and formed into objects and lives. *Yin* is the receptive and *Yang* the active principle, seen in all forms of change and difference such as the annual cycle (winter and summer), the landscape (north- facing shade and south-facing brightness), sexual coupling (female and male), the formation of both women and men as characters and sociopolitical history (disorder and order)." This dualism is further described as the "dark-bright", "negative- positive", "masculine-feminine", "winter-summer".

In Frankl's article, "Between stimulus and response, there is a space. In that space is our power to choose our response", Viktor Frankl says that there is a space between the trigger and one's response to the trigger. This space would be equivalent to the feminine and intuitive.

David R. Hawkins calls this realm The Radiant Divinity that is simultaneously 'within' and 'without', and simultaneously neither, yet both, applies to the duality yet complementary energies.

A good start for us would be to define the masculine and feminine energies, and then be introspect and honest about where we are overdeveloped, underdeveloped, and where we can make adjustments to our thoughts, perceptions and actions. In really welcoming the feminine,

The Archetype of the Woman Protector

it means that we also trust in our very personal mystical experiences and how our inner woman leads us in every moment. This means that we can longer deny the non-physical and only consider and live in the physical. Ancient women understood these non- physical mystical experiences and moved forward confidently, without hesitation. It was expected and they were trusted to make decisions that affected the collective community – all based on how they felt and what they knew in their spirit.

When women examine themselves and move forward courageously to balance their feminine and masculine energies, life changes. There will still be resistance, internally and externally, but it is worth our dedication and perseverance. It gets easier the more we do it. We no longer become as rattled by people, their opinions, fears, limitations, and projection. We must be ever vigilant. As we transform into our highest self, we will lose friends and lovers, and sometimes family. Embrace your strength, embrace your earned valor, embrace keeping your word to yourself at all costs, embrace your innate genius, and you must wholly embrace your weirdness!

It is our job, if we desire a peaceful life and harmony within ourselves, that we learn to balance the 'doing' with the 'being' parts of ourselves.

Spirituality Within Movement

My lifetime immersion of athletic and dance movements has allowed me to effortlessly alternate between the masculine and feminine physical expressions of energy. I just never knew that these movements were giving me clarity, healing, and power. It would only make sense that I am a warrior arts teacher, self-defense instructor, and metaphysician today.

There are many styles of martial arts today. Spirituality in external martial arts seems paradoxical. How can training in violent activity possibly lead to increased awareness and spiritual advancement? This has always been an Eastern belief, but now it appears that this might become a Western belief as well.

History is rich with examples of highly evolved spiritual beings who chose to be fierce warriors.

In the Hawaiian culture, *kauna* means the hidden meaning. I think of *kauna* when I think of spirituality and healing hidden within movement, and that our spirituality and healing evolve in hiding as we move. I also think of *kauna* when spirituality is disregarded as being a part of martial arts studies. It is true, though, that some only choose to work physical techniques.

Deepak Chopra said, "If we understand spirituality not as some kind of religious dogma or ideology but as the domain of awareness where we experience values like truth, goodness, beauty, love and compassion, and also intuition, creativity, insight and focused attention."

The Physics of Movement

If movement is medicine, it would be wise to know a little more about what type of medicine you are running through your body when you engage in movement.

The physics of movement is very much like the physics of nature. While discussing the physics of energy, I often use the analogy of water in a spring. Dr. Chen-Whatley says it beautifully in the next paragraph. Through the water spring's seasonal cycle, the energy converts from one form to another - between potential energy at the stationary ends of the spring to kinetic. Energy is not created or destroyed. It transfers from one state to another, much like water. Water can be gaseous, liquid, or solid. It seems that the greater feminine energy (potential or stored energy) there is in an object, the greater the masculine energy (action or kinetic energy).

Metaphysician, Dr. Caroline Chen-Whatley says, "At rest, the spring has a great deal of potential energy which is stored but not yet utilized. As the spring is set in motion, the potential energy changes to kinetic. Through its cycle, the energy is constantly cycling between potential energy at the stationary ends of the spring to kinetic. This ease and flow of energy within nature exemplifies the non-destructive properties of energy. Energy isn't simply created; it's transferred from one state to another. The greater the potential energy of an object, the greater the kinetic." Potential energy being feminine energy and kinetic energy being masculine.

This example of the energetic ebb and flow shows the purposeful, productive, and constructive energy.

Feminine and Masculine Energies in Movement

Feminine and masculine energies are displayed in forms of physical movement, from dance to sports. The feminine energy in the physical body can be seen as the focused and strategic wind up in the pitch in baseball, the path of the block or set up of a strike in martial arts forms or fighting; in the process of a leg lift in ballet, the swing wind up of a golfer, the wind back for the hockey player, or the drawback for a conversion kick or even the quarterback's wind up to throw a pass in American football.

The masculine energy can be seen as the energy released in a pitch, the full expression of the block or punch in martial arts, the fully extended leg lift in ballet, the swing of a golfer or hockey player, the point of contact with the ball by the punter, or release of the pass by the quarterback in football. Feminine and masculine energies are displayed in all forms of physical movement, from dance to sports.

Of course, masculine energy should be accessed while in a violent or life-threatening situation. But it is an energy that should also be accessed daily for everyday things. It is determining the proportionate level of masculine energy that is needed for each task.

Masculine energy balances and heals us, not just feminine energy.

This includes developing one's balanced protector energy through martial arts – internal and external - hula dance, and other physical movements. Movement changes our physical, emotional, and mental states. It acts as a form of medicine and can shift our energy in as little as five minutes.

We know that these forms of energy are not only complementary but are interconnected and interdependent in the natural world. Our motion is always shifting between potential (feminine) and kinetic (masculine) energy. If we can learn to harness, focus, and use these different expressions of energy, this would make even the smallest movements quite powerful. Outside of movement, transferring this same principle to our lives, a simple metaphysical decision could become quite powerful.

Energies in Movement

Mental and Spiritual Health through Movement

"Movement is a medicine for creating change in a person's physical, emotional, and mental states." – Carol Welch

A man who struggled daily with anxiety had witnessed a horrible attack. As his post-traumatic stress disorder and anger grew, he vowed to never be in that situation. He began to train in martial arts. As he committed to his training, his anger and post- traumatic stress disorder began to lessen. "Movement and martial arts help the practitioner to gain self-confidence through the learned assertiveness and learning to set and maintain boundaries."

No longer are Eastern mystical practices considered esoteric or reserved for only a chosen few. This is now openly discussed in practice in movement modalities - like yoga, martial arts, dance, art, and music (including drumming). We can see the steady spread of influence of spiritual principles throughout the United States and the world. This really isn't a surprise as institutionalized religions continue to increase in polarizing fanaticism and divisiveness.

Iulius-Cezar Macarie authored a beautiful piece on the exposure of systematic martial arts from the East to the West, and how martial arts became an important part of mental health, specifically in psychotherapy. He states that psychotherapists "Considered the psychotherapeutic aspects of martial arts practice and its value to verbal psychotherapy... Both disciplines seek to gain an understanding of one's character with the aim of growth toward a new and stronger way of being in the world." Other researchers such as Richman and Rehberg believe that a martial arts 'master' or 'instructor' are like that of a psychotherapist or psychoanalyst."

There is no "one-size-fits-all" checklist for life, or only one path up the mountain. For those that judge and are critical of others, knowingly or unknowingly, are the ones that really need to connect with Source and themselves. We focus on ourselves, silencing anything that does not come from within us.

Duality of Energy

Movement, any kind of movement, is a potent form of medicine that calls us to be aware of our body, mind, and spirit connection.

For some it is all about the body getting a workout, checking out mentally, and doing the same chronic moves that eventually land us to the surgery table. On the other hand, movement is about cohesiveness between the body, mind, and spirit. It calls us to use intentful movement as time to reflect on the flow and quality of one's life by the quieting and focusing of the mind, the expansion of the spirit, and to respect, honor, and move things out of the body. There is no 'right' or 'wrong' movement to accomplish this connection and self- consideration. However, there are movements that will increase your abilities to be an effective protector.

If your spirit could benefit from quiet and introspective time then yoga, internal martial arts, swimming, a Goddess walk, light hike or dancing, gardening, raking leaves, and archery would be good options.

If your spirit seeks joy then upbeat dance, jumping movements, trampoline or rebounding, light jog, core bodyweight movements, Zumba, and Jazzercise would be good options.

If your spirit seeks to clear confusion or anger then challenging HIIT, boxing, kickboxing, external martial arts, high-impact cardio, circuit-training, kettlebell, powerlifting, running, and advanced body weight exercises would be good options.

Martial Arts and the Protector

When I write about martial arts, I am not writing about the sport martial arts, such as tournament competitions, mixed martial arts, or even earning a Black Belt. I am writing about the cultural and philosophical systems and the beliefs, practices, and way of life that takes a lifetime to become physically proficient and spiritually evolved using martial arts as the vehicle for the protector's path. With the right teacher and art, martial arts studies provide discipline, physical conditioning, knowledge of the anatomy for effectiveness, mental persistence, spiritual power, endurance, balance, flexibility, quickness, and physical strength.

Martial arts are spiritual and contribute to mental health.

The profession of psychotherapy has benefited greatly by using martial arts as therapy. An account is given of a man who, once committed to his training, experienced a lessening of anger, post- traumatic stress disorder, assertiveness, and increased confidence.

The inner dimension of Asian martial arts can be related to the suffix "*Do*": Judo, Taekwondo (Korean), Aikido (Japanese), Hapkido (Korean), Karate-do (Japanese and Chinese). *Do* is derived from the Chinese word *Tao*, which in this case is a 'way' and very much an inner way. Traditionally when someone studied martial arts, they were doing two things - learning a fighting technique and learning how to gain mastery over their own self through this technique.

Gichin Funakoshi, a Japanese Karate Grandmaster, said that the ultimate aim of one's study is not the victor or loser, but to perfect one's character.

With the spiritual intention of practicing hard mental and physical training, which is *shugyo* in Japanese, the practitioners naturally developed their spirit. It is believed that the students were able to gain increased insight into the essence of reality.

"Such training continues today, but enlightenment does not occur while relaxing and contemplating the true nature of life and death; it only occurs through dedicated training and unwavering perseverance."

"Some martial arts traditions maintain a system of ethics and honor and pursue a path of self- mastery. Others emphasize combat, competition, and fighting. Being a fighter does not make one a spiritual warrior. The battle of the spiritual warrior is the mastery of oneself."

The Dalai Lama, and authors Haruki Murakami and M. Kathleen Casey have a mantra, "Pain is inevitable. Suffering is optional". If we choose a significant other who does not suffer well, our lives and purpose will be dramatically impacted, if not thwarted entirely. Through our growth and freedom, in this space between pain and response, is our power to choose.

"Martial arts are a spiritual challenge, not a physical one." **Ronny Yu**

Before we can ready our bodies for more power, we must first overcome our mind and its limiting beliefs. We must overcome the belief that we: (1) are a victim or prey; (2) will be or continue to be a victim because we have already experienced a violent or sexual experience and have PTSD and have been unable heal; and (3) we could never, ever, win against a man.

Once we believe we are worth the fight, that we are worth protecting - even if it costs us our life - the body then follows the mind's belief. This is where we now begin to step into our power - mentally, spiritually, and physically. When we learn how to protect ourselves, it brings confidence, and confidence brings peace of mind that lessens fear and paranoia.

Martial arts prepare one's entire being to recognize and embrace Divine energy. In Hawaiian, this is called *mana*. In Indian, it is called *prana*. In Chinese, it is called *chi*. But in Hawaiian, *mana* encompasses more than the limited English definition of just energy or power. Mary Pukui says *mana* is "power possessed by man, but originating in the supernatural, and thus always imbued with a mystic quality."

Rev. Dr. William Wong, ND, PhD says that when one is deep into martial training, one is exposed to realms that feel three-dimensional. Wong said, "This knowledge expanded their knowledge of themselves and how they fit into The One (the Tao, Nirvana, Universe, the Creator, God, Akua). Some gifted monks, after much practice, could achieve temporary absorption into the essence of the Creator (known in Western Mysticism as the Mystical Union)." Contrary to what some believe about external martial arts, this leaves students feeling expanded - mentally and spiritually – with inner acceptance, peace, love, and wisdom.

Adam Brady, a martial artist and teacher of yoga, believes we exist in our physical anatomy (confined to the physical level) and that non- physical energy centers channel through the spinal column, even though this life energy does not exist within the physical body. Adam uses the analogy of energy centers being rooms in our house. Within each room we typically accomplish different things: we cook in the kitchen, we sleep in the bedroom, we relax in the living room, and we clean ourselves in the bathroom. Higher awareness and self-fulfillment happen when mapping the energy center system with martial arts training.

Divine energy is an experience that one never forgets. This energy recenters, programs, and heals. But one has to move in order to experience it. It feels like a fleeting yet never-ending flash of time where you transparently commune with Divinity; where revelation, clarity, and power gently surge through all one's senses and systems. In this moment, however short or long, it never feels long enough. So, we keep moving and look forward to having this deep connection again – the feeling of connection that we can truly only feel while in movement.

The Archetype of the Woman Protector

Honor and self-mastery have everything to do with being a protector – whether physical, metaphysical, or both. It is the path to prepare the body for increased Divine energy. Attaining a level of proficiency in training can differ 180-degrees between the sexes.

I spoke with one of few remaining master elders of the only native warrior art, *Ku'ialua* (*"Lua"*) of the People of Hawai'i. This elder said that training in *Lua* is, in this order - techniques, conditioning, and then the mind. Through the training of a brutal joint dislocation combat art, a man gained conditioning, and then control of his mind. I find this to be true after training for 25 years under one male master teacher, being trained as one of the men.

However, for most other women, this is not the desired path. The path is opposite of men. They learn the techniques, condition, then gain belief. From what I have witnessed, most women must first believe, condition, then learn the techniques. Most non-martial women will put anything and anyone else before their training. Self-importance, declared intention, and laser-focus are paramount to women that dedicate to regular training. Knowing the difference in how we each learn helps us to seek out the proper teachers, proper information for each purpose, not give up too quickly, and to give ourselves the permission and freedom to welcome the regular learnings and our unique path in mastering the learnings.

Adaptability

Each situation is different and constantly developing. Our intellect and intuition are necessary if we wish to make a healthy and educated decision. I always say life is like a martial arts technique. You wouldn't use the same defense against a 280-pound 6'0" opponent as you would against a 190-pound 6'4" opponent. Such is life. We adjust as needed to be successful and learn the lesson that presents itself through each situation.

Besides increasing our relationship with ourselves (therefore Source) and the confidence we gain from our training, we need to be able to mentally step back, evaluate, make our decision, take the correct actions, and be at peace with our action (even if our action is silence). In training and in life, anxiety is caused by not accepting where we are and where we think we should be or do. During martial arts *hula* or *kata* (martial forms), we must have a quiet and focused mind. Training techniques or while conditioning requires us to be in the present moment through focus on our breath, balance, and movements. Training with partners also helps us to stay focused.

Bunkai Jitsu says, "When practicing *kata*/ patterns/ forms we focus not only on the pattern of movements but our balance, posture, body structures and mechanics, efficient generation of power, breathing and knowing where every part of our body is at any given time. With practice we develop a great degree of body awareness. As mind and body are linked, body awareness helps to develop mental awareness."

Science proves that mental health is affected by neurotransmitters – Anandamide, Serotonin, and Norepinephrine. In addition to igniting and balancing your brain chemistry, consistent endorphins from regular training also increase our mental health. This comes with lovely byproducts like weight loss, reduced fear of attack, increased confidence, and belonging to a like-minded group wherein we find support and community.

> *"There is not an anti-depressant that will cure a depression that is spiritually based."*
> *– David R. Hawkins*

This is Metaphysical!

Some cultural martial arts have a healing element. The Japanese say *satsu/katsu* that it is the 'life taking' and 'life giving' should be part of the one's martial arts studies.

David Brown says, "There is always a time for warrior energy; the warrior should cut in and out of her energy as required without any shame or guilt, while recognizing her own space, her own truth, and her own personal power. To fully welcome that power when she does what is right for herself, through courageous strength and action. To use this action energy to release any trauma or disease that has been stored in our bodies." This is metaphysical!

Since the movie, *The Last Samurai*, the traditional practice of martial arts has people

realizing that esoteric spiritual belief structures are deeper within most martial arts. It is nice to see the evolution of the deeper martial arts meaning of self-mastery be acknowledged as a tool for spiritual growth. Not just acknowledged, but that martial arts were believed to be formed to awaken the deep spirit within." This is metaphysical!

Maurice Zalle says that "He who wishes to live in an oriental martial art, rather than to just practice it on a physical level, must so train his consciousness to attain a self-discipline that at last his conscious mind will merge into an identity with the very principle of life itself." This is metaphysical!

A Taoist and Buddhist-based internal martial art system of *Baguazhang* was made for alignment and healing of the mind, physical, spiritual bodies through a higher consciousness. It is believed to be "one of the greatest tools to find balance in the war inside and out." This is metaphysical!

The *Tai Chi* and *Xingyi* internal martial arts systems provide for greater connection with one's internal anatomy, flow of "*Qi*", and one's peaceful nature through mastery of the inner spirit through physical movement and breath. This is metaphysical!

The Archetype of the Woman Protector

Arnis-Escrima is the Filipino external martial art that has the internal healing art, *Hilot*, within. *Hilot* is one of the three main branches of Philippine healing tradition. Filipino folk healers were generally categorized into three divisions—the *manghihilot*, the *albolaryo*, and the *kumadrona* or *partera*. Perry Gil S. Mallari says his late uncle and *manghihilot* (a *Hilot* practitioner), Penitente G. Apolinar, used his hand freely and never claimed to have had any contact with any mystical beings. He did say that when healing his patients that one must intend it to happen. This is metaphysical!

Master Lao Shir Cynthia Ming believes that practicing *Tai Chi* and *Qi Gong* are the healing sisters of the Chinese martial arts. This is metaphysical!

Another martial art that incorporates healing is *Danzan Ryu*. Most practitioners at the Sensei-level are *Seifukujitsu* healers in this integrated martial- healing combination of ancient Chinese medicine, Japanese martial, and the and Japanese and Hawaiian cultural body work. It incorporates deep tissue style bodywork, promotes, and improves blood and *qi* circulation, strengthening the body's energy systems, and rapidly assists with injuries. This is metaphysical!

Internal *Qigong* ("*Chi Kung*") is mainly used for introspection, evolution, and the prevention of physical diseases. A dedicated practitioner has been known to prolong life and reduce body weight. The external *Qigong* is mainly used to enhance one's physical power and accuracy. This is metaphysical!

Metaphysical Protector Energy

Metaphysical protection is necessary when confronted with non- or pre-physical threats and attacks. Some ways we can protect our spirit and energy bodies are to set our intentions for the day and to ask for increased protection. We do this by recommitting to our purpose and reinstating our intentions throughout the day. Expressing gratitude at the end of the day and asking for messages while we sleep. It is important to have a gifted healer who can clear energies that insist on affecting us that we are unable to clear on our own.

I encounter people who seek the Eastern disconnection way of detachment while others seek the Western narcissistic way of attachment. Either way may feel imbalanced as they limit our communication with ourselves, Source, and others.

Discussing and studying the physical self is a part of psychology, psychoanalysis, behaviorism, humanism, and others. Part of these human studies is the practice of metaphysical self-defense. Without it, we can be affected in our moods, emotions, speech, and how we feel physically (stomach issues, headaches, throat, breathing issues, etc.).

The Archetype of the Woman Protector

Metaphysical women protectors also use prayer, petition, ceremony and to ask for assistance when a little backup is needed. This is invaluable when we are feeling incoming energy and addressing psychic vampires or predators. I believe that the effectiveness of our discussions with the non- physical are increased when we call upon Source for increased guidance and protection.

There are some people who also attempt to try to influence us psychically in a conscious way. This influence does not require these people to be in your presence. They can be fixated on you, an argument, or an event that you were a part of, or they merely dislike your latest social media post. This energy directed towards you could be a thought or verbal comment made that can swing to the other end of the energy spectrum to obsessive fixation.

This focus conjures destructive energy, and its target is you.

Not surprising, the potency and effect of this destructive energy is offset by the protective and loving energy that others think about or directly send to you.

The general phrase of this destructive energy is a "psychic attack", which I have personally experienced and continue to experience. Most times physical events manifest out of these psychic attacks. They come in the form of inexplicable physical body issues and injuries, "accidents", electronic interference, car problems, missing items (i.e., keys, wallet), and unprovoked turmoil with others.

Some things that help cancel out or minimize the frequency and strength of these attacks are:

Set an Intention: Say aloud that it is your intent to release or block any negative or destructive energy that is being sent to you, knowingly or unknowingly. Sometimes, when it is persistent, it is appropriate to send the energy back to its sender and call for energetic backup.

Meditation: Focus on gratitude, peace, protection, and abundance.

Movement: Any type of movement helps to move energy through your physical and energetic bodies.

White Light: The White Light protection method is the most common and popular meditation. We can do this in a waking or moving meditation, too. Visualize a white light coming down and surrounding you by covering your being making a protective shield, like you are inside an egg or a bubble or ball, where a white light surrounds you.

Elemental Protection: Visualize the elements of Earth, Water, Wood, Fire, Metal, Wind, and Air. You can imagine a wall of any of these elements, or in combination, as your psychic protection shield.

Mirror Effect: If you know that you are going to meet a negative-minded person, just imagine several mirrors surrounding you from head to toe. Imagine that all mirrors are facing away from you and towards the person you are interacting with. This way, all the negative energy released by that person will be reflected to him or her. (Much like returning the energy to the sender).

Salt: I use this all the time, especially while traveling the world to teach. Salt is the most common method across all the world's belief systems to absorb and restrict negative energy and the negative intentions of others. I use sea salt from Hawai'i. You can use it in a bath, along windowsills and doorways, and can place some in your mouth if you are suddenly and inexplicably not feeling well.

Prayer or Ritual: Prayer, ritual, or asking for assistance, is indispensable when addressing psychic vampires or predators, or when you feel an unwelcoming energetic presence. Clear your space of energy not at the vibrational level of Love.

Physical Protector Energy

Protector energy manifests in choice, words, actions, and behaviors. Protector energy also ignites when we are about to engage in a physical altercation, a fall or collision, or anything physical that is unexpected and not desired.

There are irrefutable benefits from choosing to use protector energy, appropriately and regularly, so that we are prepared for when this protector energy begins to surge. In my experience, the choice to use protector energy takes intimacy with this energetic vibration that reverberates throughout your entire body. If we are not used to feeling it, we will freeze when confronted with incoming action energy (force) in physical form.

To practice using this intense and fluctuating energy, start by acknowledging and accepting what it feels like, then harness it, begin to try to focus it, and use it. This means to feel it flow throughout your physical being; to embrace it and not suppress it; to then breathe into it and focus; to use it to strategically train in movement – whether it is yoga, dance, martial arts, archery, sports, etc. Get out of your head and into your body!

It is in physical movement where true transformation occurs.

If we can become 'one' with the opposite end of the spectrum of energy (masculine/action), where few voluntarily choose to go, we are imbalanced and not moving towards our full potential. Moreover, we are wasting energy that is presenting itself for us to manipulate and use!

My female relative has said, "I would rather have a root canal than take a [physical] self-defense workshop."

Earlier we discussed the usage of the word "warrior." Well, "self-defense" is another one of these words that has a very poor connotation and for good reason.

The Archetype of the Woman Protector

Usually when we hear "self-defense" we immediately get a vision of a highly confident man with a 20th Degree Black Belt (or Red Belt these days) to show us 'helpless women' how to defend against a potential physical attack. Thankfully not all male self-defense instructors are of this stereotype as some truly wish to empower women as if we were their family. However, it is very common thus why it is a stereotype that exists. Comedy routines are made about this sort of Supreme Greatest Grandmaster.

When I hear a male instructor say, "You *just* do this ..." Anytime I hear the word "just" used, implying simplicity, I cringe. It is usually followed up with, "That's all you need to do. BAM! BOOM! You've taken him out!" More and more everyday women, young women's organizations, women experiencing homelessness, at universities, adult entertainers, and health care associations seek a competent woman self-defense instructor for this very reason.

This is where protector energy comes into play - trained or untrained. The common responses to an assault (defined as the belief of imminent physical danger) are fight, flight, freeze, fawn (compliance while timing your response). The fight-flight- freeze-fawn response is the body's natural reaction to danger and our reaction to threats - like an oncoming car, or a growling or charging dog.

The response instantly shocks the nervous system and causes physiological changes in our adrenal, hormonal, visual, and respiratory systems. Adrenaline surges for 30-45 seconds with effects lasting much longer. Our hippocampus shrinks as our amygdala enlarges. This causes our vision to become tunneled and our hearing becomes impaired.

Our effectiveness in protecting ourselves, and others, is based on our awareness of a developing situation and how we react.

The benefits of learning self-protection are many. Some of the benefits are safety, street awareness, our ability to protect ourselves and our loved ones; increased self-confidence; increased mental health; improved focus; improved ability to handle emotions and physiological effects during an incident; increased fitness, balance, self-discipline, and a protector's quick reflex.

Protection – Metaphysical and Physical

While we have been taught that self-protection primarily applies to physical incidents, I propose that it applies to all attacks – metaphysical and physical - including mental and financial. This is war from the protector's perspective. How we prepare before the battle, and how and when we respond, determines our success with minimizing collateral damage to ourselves and others.

As we educate and train ourselves in protector energy, this protects us.

The Archetype of the Woman Protector

All forms of self-protection are equally important. Initially this training is uncomfortable. We get triggered and, in that energy - we feel it, learn how to embrace it, focus it, and use it by moving into action. This causes our fight-flight- freeze-fawn to no longer be an unconscious decision. We gain control. We train to know how we will respond when a situation presents itself, and we will respond the same way as we train.

There are different ways to define these areas of self-protection, protection against us (what?!) and protection against others.

Metaphysical Protection could be defined as: Internal – Unconscious belief systems (neurological programming) that we have running that are not beneficial to us and strongly influence our perception, or in the least, affects our essence.

External - Protecting our mind (and subsequent emotions) from attacks from destructive energy that shows up in our energetic field or is being sent to us - knowingly or unknowingly - by someone else. Metaphysical self-protection is to protect against energetic beings or entities, not physical people.

Physical Protection could be defined as:

Internal – Habits and behaviors that harm our physical and energetic bodies through self-harm like cutting, substance abuse, consistent harmful self-talk and criticism, and lack of anything the body needs (nutrition, sleep, rest, and hydration).

External - Awareness and saying something or doing something that provides physical protection of self or others.

Mental Protection could be defined as:
Internal - Awareness that our internal
'Predator' needs to be silenced and we need to take control over our thoughts. Our thoughts produce correlating emotions which can make you ill and ruin relationships and reputations.
External - Someone is attempting to manipulate and play mind games with you.

Financial Protection could be defined as:

Internal - When we have the chronic behavior of sabotaging our financial stability through lack of discipline, depleting our financial energy, have emotionally driven spending, or provide financial assistance to others when it complicates or harms our own livelihood.

External – Someone, intentionally or unintentionally, is threatening our financial livelihood and stability.

All these areas of self-protection overlap as we are energetically made up of body, mind, and spirit.

"You're not on a path. You are the path."

The Archetype of the Woman Protector

Women have always had the advantage. We have just forgotten, but it is locked within our DNA. In the pre-contact Hawaiian culture, men had to invoke the presence and wisdom of Divinity through *hula* (dance), *ho'okupu* (gifts), and *mōhai* (sacrifices). Women did not as they were seen as directly connected to *Pō* (Divinity) - who were made to and operated as a portal of the non-physical realm into to the physical realm. Women were not to be spiritually defiled by participating in the physical ways and duties of terrestrial man.

Although different, and with different responsibilities, both men and women were equal and respected. In our Western world, the new evolved word "telestial" would now apply to women and men. Telestial, a combination of celestial and terrestrial to obviously mean both from God, far away, distant, heaven, sky (celestial) and of earth, ground (terrestrial).

I believe our protector foremothers would be classified today as metaphysician-warriors or protectors. This means that as protectors, they were metaphysical *and* physical, balanced in both, not one or the other. Our imbalanced patriarchal society of male dominance, male identification, and male centeredness has some wondering if our courageous warrior foremothers even existed at all.

In today's world, any extreme belief has destructive outcomes. The extreme feminist movement is remarkable;

however, it can be toxic, too, equally if not more harmful than patriarchy. I say this because feminism may contain, within it, toxic beliefs such as women unconsciously (and sadly consciously) operating in the ingrained prejudice against other women and blanket hatred for men. This is presently called internalized misogyny that only continues the longstanding patriarchy of oppression and shame associated with being a woman, by women towards women.

Any toxic masculinity and toxic femininity within us would be eradicated by us operating in our protector energy.

There are many real-life accounts of a women protectors. Sara Keller Lozen, nicknamed the 'Apache Joan of Arc", was a 19th century Chiricahua or Warm Springs Apache warrior and metaphysical leader. It was said that Lozen had the strength of a man, was a cunning military strategist, was highly proficient in matters of medicine, was braver than most, and would act as a shield for her people. The Legend of Lozen says that her metaphysical abilities helped her form her military strategies and to detect enemy movement.

Many protectors weren't just highly skilled physically, they were also highly in-tune to the non- physical. Today these protectors would be considered diviners, shaman, mystics, or even craftswomen. Like the Scottish

The Archetype of the Woman Protector

metaphysician- warrior, *Scáthach*, a martial arts warrior, master teacher of men, weapons maker, seer, and priestess.

We are being offered the opportunity to honor our spiritual lineage of sacred work as inheritors and guardians as protectors.

If we choose, we get to be a part of the restoration of protector work in this generation and future generations, to impact the balance and healing of Mother Earth's energies, and to serve Source by serving our communities. If we choose to access and use our protector energy, it will require us to use our intellect and intuition to regularly examine our behaviors, our relationships, and our purpose. To adapt and move into action.

It is my strong belief that we can live fully by using both intellect and intuition consistently, not having to be only one of these aspects. We are not just "beauty, brains, or brawn." It is a constant challenge to help the world see our fullness as women, but it can be difficult when media continues to display these as separate qualities, exacerbated by TV shows pitting one woman up against another. We experience enough woman-on- woman hate on a daily basis.

Dr. Catherine Collautt says that "A metaphysician [spiritual protector] is either a philosopher whose area of expertise is the study of the fundamental nature of reality and existence and/ or, more esoterically, a practicing healer/

adviser that changes physical reality by working with the principles and powers and 'things' that underlie it, and especially the mind or psyche".

If we do not take regular self-inventory, we don't know what our essence is. Our essence determines everything.

Essence > Perception > Options > Choices > Words > Actions > Behaviors > Destiny

Who we are determines how we see things. How we see things determines what options are available to us. We can then make choices based on our options. Our choices determine our words and actions. Our consistent words and actions become our behaviors. Our behaviors become the quality and fulfillment in our life - our destiny.

A protector prepares and strategizes in the feminine energy, then moves into action through masculine energy. A protector uses, equally, her intellect and her intuition, and works equally in the physical and non-physical realms.

Embracing the Role of Protector

A woman protector knows most times that battle is unnecessary. Most of us train so we don't have to engage. This is in both the physical and the spiritual realms.

Relying on our spirit, women protectors make instant moral judgments and behave accordingly, most times

The Archetype of the Woman Protector

realizing there is no battle – or that, it is not the protector's battle but belongs to someone else.

A woman protector holds few fixed viewpoints and is flexible and adaptable. We are free to not judge too quickly, yet quickly know what must be done, when and how. We are blessed with this gift.

We are independent yet can seamlessly be a part of a like-minded tribe.

A woman protector is self-accountable for her choices and actions, displaying compassion, empathy, and understands pain and consequences.

A woman protector does not seek out or provoke war.

A woman protector should never save others from their own wars as it is part of their path, not hers.

The Divine Feminine is nurturing, intuitive, and forgiving, but it is also fearless, powerful, alchemic, magnetic, fierce, and sometimes vicious. As spiritual protectors we must have wisdom, and not get distracted or step off our path and into what is supposed to be a lesson for someone else.

If a protector responds, she is connected to the intuitive and dedicates herself to exude great wisdom, strategy, skill, timing, and appropriate intensity.

"Warriors use their intent and will to shape their lives. All of their actions are conscious, intentional, and complete."
– **Kerr Cuhulain**

The Modern Protector

What does it mean to be a protector in modern times? One meaning, these days, isn't sufficient. Some say it is any woman who overcomes extreme hardship, one who advocates for the resources and rights of others, one who works to rescue and protect others, one who defends core feminine values, one who serves in their country's military, one who is a sport fighting athlete, one who impacts the world under tremendous adversity, one who changed the course of history, and more. For the purposes of this book, it is a woman that is equally working in both the spiritual and physical realms by using intellect and intuition and is physically trained to protect.

Any of the above definitions will encounter external criticism and resistance. It only matters how you define being a protector. Internal resistance is when we are unsure of our tendencies and therefore our path. Some will deem it too difficult and continue to harness and operate in patriarchal power or only in the intellect. We have been led to believe that we need to operate in patriarchal ways to survive in today's world; to become exactly what we have survived. Then there are the women who have the opposite reaction and avoid the masculine energy altogether.

The Archetype of the Woman Protector

There are women who do not know the difference between masculine energy and patriarchal energy.

There are several quotes I am disgusted by. The first is, "*She is just a man without a penis.*" The second is, "*She has penis envy.*" I consistently see women that step into their rightful space and are labeled as toxic, aggressive, and power hungry. None of us wish to be labeled as such, so we dim our voices, contributions, actions, and visibility.

Unfortunately, this still happens to us in corporate America and in martial arts.

Women embody masculine energy, just as men embody feminine energy. There is a difference between healthy masculine energy and patriarchal energy. Patriarchal energy is about power, heterosexual dominance, gender superiority, and control. We also see this displayed within toxic feminine energy operating as disguised patriarchal energy that devalue females (of all ages) and lies at the core of gender-based inequality and violence. Patriarchy is a structural force in society that influences power relations, whether they are abusive or not.

We now see men born as men that identify as women, and women born as women identifying as men. This discussion is not about gender, it is about the physics of energy and how we can use energy in our lives. The feminine energy known for its coiled, potential, and strategic set-up; the frozen water, if you will. As the feminine starts to thaw and take kinetic motion, it converts into the masculine energy of action. Neither can exist, in an energy sense, without the other. Equal and opposite.

This not only applies in the physical realm of body movements, but also in the metaphysical realm in balancing one's life and spirit with connection to Source. One cannot rely solely on one's intellect and 'thinkingness'. To have self- evolution and make truly educated decisions, one must equally use the masculine (intellect) and the feminine (intuition). This requires one to think and to feel, not one or the other. This is the way of the woman protector.

"There is a voice that doesn't use words, listen." – **Rumi**

Conclusion

"For all I know, I know nothing if I cannot demonstrate a better life."
– **Dr. Paul Masters**

The material discussed, academic research examined, and my life experience has and continues to shape the path of my truth and purpose.

Each of us must move through the unknown to remove distractions and things we allow to hold us back from experiencing and achieving. It is our choice on how we move through fear, challenges, stagnation, and resistance using psychic, physical, and spiritual movement.

The Archetype of the Woman Protector

The woman protector is nothing new. This important archetype has always existed. She exists now and there are more in training and awakening to this fact. This archetype exudes all that is a protector in the physical and non-physical realms.

As protectors we set our intention, develop our metaphysical connections and experiences, train and care for our physicality, and remain in purpose and action. We are as much a spiritual protector as we are a physical protector.

Women protectors know in their core that using their intellect and intuition will bring freedom. We learn to show gratitude for the lessons that our traumatic experiences have brought and finally, and fully, step into connection with ourselves. In taking control over our thoughts we can heal, re-form, strengthen, and evolve our beliefs. In reforming our belief systems, we create communion with ourselves and have very personal mystical experiences with Source to help guide and affirm us. We find peace and freedom by relying on our trusted intuition.

In creating peace and freedom within us, we live in the present moment of awareness as our celestial team helps to clear our path to enjoy the present and prepare for the future. We fully embrace what we are... the Creator of our life experience.

Life is happening *for* me, not *to* me.

Scáthach owned her sovereignty, as did all our protector foremothers. May we welcome, embrace, and own our sovereignty. May we fulfill our divine purpose by applying metaphysical principles and protector energy. May we embrace our life's purpose, in physical form and in all other realms in which we exist. Let us birth and nurture our dreams and purpose into existence, from the spiritual realm into the physical realm.

Steven Pressfield said, "Every breath we take, every heartbeat, every evolution of every cell comes from God and is sustained my God every second, just as every creation, invention, every bar of music or line of verse, every thought, vision, fantasy, every dumb-ass flop and stroke of genius comes from that infinite intelligence that created us and the universe in all its dimensions, out of the Void, the field of infinite potential, primal chaos, the muse. To acknowledge that reality, to efface all ego, to let the work come through us and give it back freely to its source, that, in my opinion, is as true to reality as it gets."

"Neo, sooner or later you're going to realize, just as I did, there's a difference between knowing the path and walking the path." – **Morpheus in** *The Matrix*

About the Author

Dr. Kumu Michelle Manu, JD, PhD, a multi-disciplinarian, is the Founder and Curator of a dynamic women's movement, Sovereign Woman Collective. Her unique approach to total wellness, self-protection, and cultivated freedom has been actively utilized to empower women to gain or regain their inherent right to govern themselves.

Michelle accepts offers to work regularly in the entertainment industry in TV shows, films, podcasts, and live television. She has credits as producer, director, host, fight actress, and fight coordinator in several films, series, and projects.

Dr. Manu is a published author, including titles *The Archetype of the Woman Protector* and *The Butterfly Effect*.

Dr. Manu is internationally known for her accomplishments as a 10th Degree Black Belt, *Alihikaua* (General), and *Kumu Lua* (teacher) of the indigenous Hawaiian cultural warrior art, the *Lua* (Kaihewalu and Manu lineages). Kumu Manu is the only high-ranking female teacher of this art and the only public representative of a Hawaiian woman warrior in over 200 years. She is the only woman to be honored with the designation of *Knight Commander* of the Royal Order of Kamehameha I (O'ahu Chapter), for her continued work in protecting, promoting, and perpetuating the Hawaiian culture through the *Lua*.

Kumu Manu toured the Midwest as a professional Polynesian *Hula* dancer and choreographer for ten years. She empowers thousands of women using the *Hula* dance to teach *Lua*. She believes it is essential for timing, balance, placement, and biomechanics during close-quarters combat. Using this proven method, Kumu Manu teaches internationally at UCLA and Honolulu Community College, and privately at her school *Nā Koa/Pā Lua O Manu*.

Using the *Lua* and *Hula*, Kumu Manu teaches self-protection to people in high-risk environments such as pilots and flight attendants, real estate professionals, healthcare professionals, university students, adult entertainers, women experiencing domestic violence and homelessness, and women working in many other industries. Kumu Manu requires dedicated students to study the ways of the ancient warrior: metaphysical science, warrior massage, wellness and conditioning.

Dr. Manu has been a legal professional for three decades. She earned a Juris Doctorate (JD), business credentials from George Washington University, leadership for senior executives credential from Harvard Business School, a master's degree in Metaphysical Science (MMsc), and a doctorate in Philosophy specializing in metaphysical counseling.

Kumu Manu is featured in magazines, including *Sports Illustrated, Black Belt Magazine, Hawaiian Airlines Hana Hou!, Martial Arts Xperience, Inside Kung Fu, Martial Arts Masters Magazine, Seni Beladiri* (Malaysia), *Tae Kwon Do Times* (Korea), *USAdojo.com, KenpoGirl, Herstory, Martial Arts Illustrated UK, Warrior Magazin*

The Archetype of the Woman Protector

(Germany), *Martial Journal*, *Immersion Labs*, and *El Camino The Way* (Spain).

Some of the noteworthy awards she has been given:
2024 Presidential Lifetime Achievement Award
2024 Person of the Year by Custom Trends Magazine
2017 Inductee Argentina Martial Arts Hall of Fame
2017 Woman of the Year Kenpo International Association
2017 Female Empowerment Inspiration by WGSC
2017 Special Celebrity by Munich Hall of Honour
2016 Knight Commander by Royal Order of Kamehameha I
2016 Hall of Fame Inductee Martial Arts History Museum
2006 Inductee Masters Hall of Fame